The Pocket Book of
Mindfulness

The Pocket Book of
Mindfulness

Live in the moment and reduce stress

ARCTURUS

ARCTURUS

This edition published in 2016 by Arcturus Publishing Limited
26/27 Bickels Yard, 151–153 Bermondsey Street,
London SE1 3HA

ISBN: 978-1-78404-473-2
AD004402NT

Printed in China

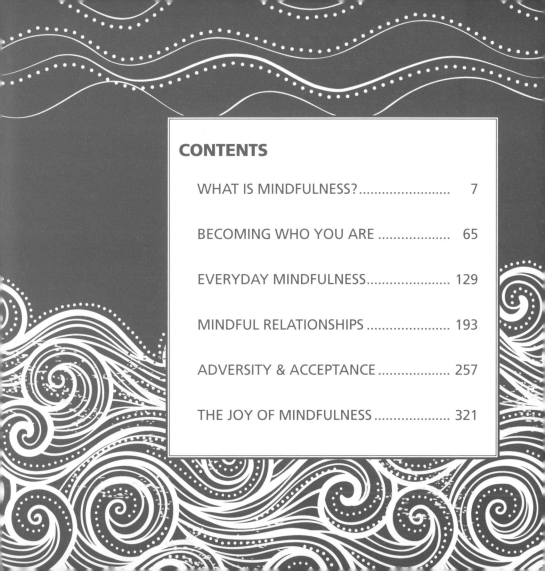

CONTENTS

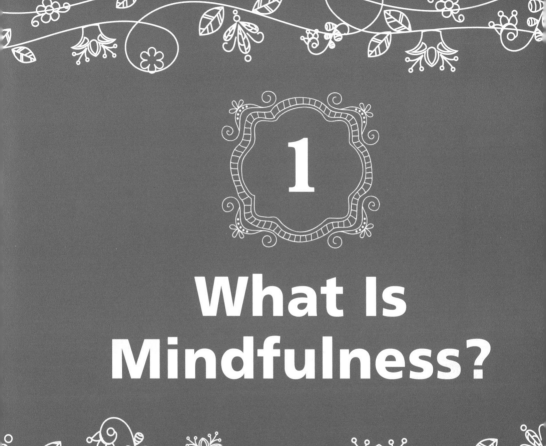

1

What Is Mindfulness?

To dwell in the here and now does not mean you never think about the past or plan responsibly for the future. The idea is simply not to allow yourself to get lost in regrets about the past or worries about the future. If you are firmly grounded in the present moment, the past can be an object of inquiry, the object of your mindfulness and concentration. You can attain many insights by looking into the past. But you are still grounded in the present moment.

Thich Nhat Hanh

Mindfulness is simply being aware of what is happening right now without wishing it were different; enjoying the pleasant without holding on when it changes (which it will); being with the unpleasant without fearing it will always be this way (which it won't).

James Baraz

Mindfulness, also called wise attention, helps us see what we're adding to our experiences, not only during meditation sessions but also elsewhere.

Sharon Salzberg

World is a dance. Mindfulness is witnessing that dance.

Amit Ray

Mindfulness is focused awareness applied to immediate experience in both its subjective and objective factors.

Bhikkhu Bodhi

Most of us take for granted that time flies, meaning that it passes too quickly. But in the mindful state, time doesn't really pass at all. There is only a single instant of time that keeps renewing itself over and over with infinite variety.

Deepak Chopra

Stay present for the 'now' of your life. It's your point of power.

Doug Dillon

It takes practice to learn how to open up each moment of your life. But we have lots of moments, and each one gives us a brand-new chance to learn again.

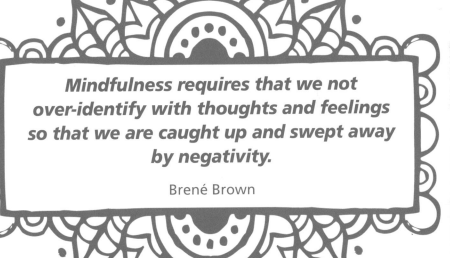

Mindfulness requires that we not over-identify with thoughts and feelings so that we are caught up and swept away by negativity.

Brené Brown

We cannot live in the past; it is gone. Nor can we live in the future; it is forever beyond our grasp. We can live only in the present.

S.N. Goenka

Mindfulness meditation doesn't change life. Life remains as fragile and unpredictable as ever. Meditation changes the heart's capacity to accept life as it is.

Sylvia Boorstein

We use mindfulness to observe the way we cling to pleasant experiences and push away unpleasant ones.

Sharon Salzberg

Through recognizing and realizing the empty essence, instead of being selfish and self-centred, one feels very open and free.

Tsoknyi Rinpoche

Our vision is more obstructed by what we think we know than by our lack of knowledge.

Kristen Stendahl

Mindfulness has never met a cognition it didn't like.

Daniel J. Siegel

Our minds are full of irritants, like fear and jealousy and greed. Mindfulness is a way of clearing our minds of such irritants.

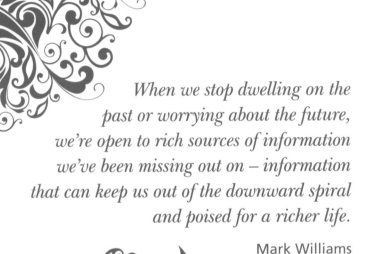

When we stop dwelling on the past or worrying about the future, we're open to rich sources of information we've been missing out on – information that can keep us out of the downward spiral and poised for a richer life.

Mark Williams

Two thoughts cannot coexist at the same time: if the clear light of mindfulness is present, there is no room for mental twilight.

Nyanaponika Thera

Mindfulness is paying attention to the right things, and paying no attention to the wrong things.

*If we are mindful, we are
aware of the tendency to first
concentrate and then to feel
anger when something interferes with
that concentration. With mindfulness
we can concentrate when it is
appropriate to do so and
not concentrate when it is
appropriate not to do so.*

Ajahn Sumedho

*Awareness in itself
is healing.*

Fritz Pearls

**To be mindful of social
phenomena is thus to
identify more clearly
hatred, greed, and
delusion as well as the
seeds of wisdom and
compassion both around
us and in us.**

Donald Rothberg

**The thoughts we choose to
think are the tools we use to
paint the canvas of our lives.**

Louise Hay

**If you really want to
remove a cloud from your
life, you do not make a big
production of it, you just
relax and remove it from
your thinking. That's all
there is to it.**

Richard Bach

*In order to sow seeds, you must
first clear a patch of land.
Mindfulness helps to clear a
space in our minds which we
can use to plant the seeds of hope
and joy in.*

We too should make ourselves empty, that the great soul of the universe may fill us with its breath.

Laurence Binyon

When we meditate we expand, spreading our wings like a bird, trying to enter consciously into Infinity, Eternity and Immortality, welcoming them into our aspiring consciousness.

Sri Chinmoy

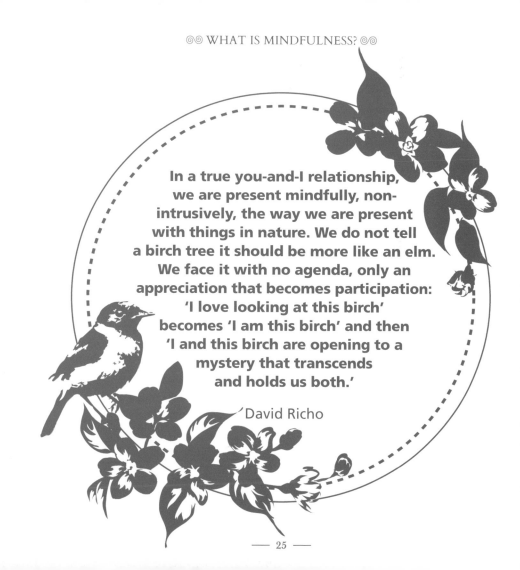

In a true you-and-I relationship,
we are present mindfully, non-
intrusively, the way we are present
with things in nature. We do not tell
a birch tree it should be more like an elm.
We face it with no agenda, only an
appreciation that becomes participation:
'I love looking at this birch'
becomes 'I am this birch' and then
'I and this birch are opening to a
mystery that transcends
and holds us both.'

David Richo

Mindfulness is not concerned with anything transcendent or divine. It serves as an antidote to theism, a cure for sentimental piety, a scalpel for excising the tumour of metaphysical belief.

Stephen Batchelor

Mindfulness provides the most simple and direct, the most thorough and effective method for training and developing the mind for its daily tasks and problems.

Nyanaponika Thera

Remember one thing: meditation means awareness. Whatsoever you do with awareness is meditation.

Osho

For me mindfulness is like building a house, so the next time the tsunami that is depression comes I'll have a structure in place to resist it.

Ruby Wax

As we encounter new experiences with a mindful and wise attention, we discover that one of three things will happen to our new experience: it will go away, it will stay the same, or it will get more intense. Whatever happens does not really matter.

Jack Kornfield

Each place is the right place – the place where I now am can be a sacred space.

Ravi Ravindra

To meditate is to listen with a receptive heart.

Shakyamuni Buddha

When we raise ourselves through meditation to what unites us with the spirit, we quicken something within us that is eternal and unlimited by birth and death. Once we have experienced this eternal part in us, we can no longer doubt its existence. Meditation is thus the way to knowing and beholding the eternal, indestructible, essential centre of our being.

Rudolf Steiner

Power is about what you can control. Freedom is about what you can unleash.

Harriet Rubin

Meditation is the ultimate mobile device; you can use it anywhere, any time, unobtrusively.

Sharon Salzberg

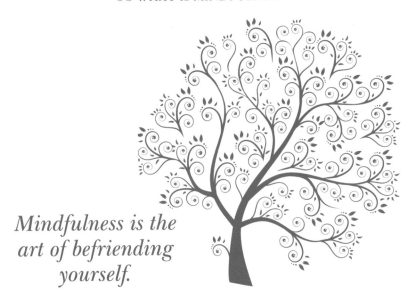

Mindfulness is the art of befriending yourself.

Not merely an absence of noise, Real Silence begins when a reasonable being withdraws from the noise in order to find peace and order in his inner sanctuary.

Peter Minard

Do not encumber your mind with useless thoughts. What good does it do to brood on the past or anticipate the future? Remain in the simplicity of the present moment.

Dilgo Khyentse Rinpoche

When you reach a calm and quiet meditative state, that is when you can hear the sound of silence.

Stephen Richards

*Feelings, whether of compassion
or irritation, should be welcomed,
recognized, and treated on an absolutely
equal basis; because both are ourselves.*

Thich Nhat Hanh

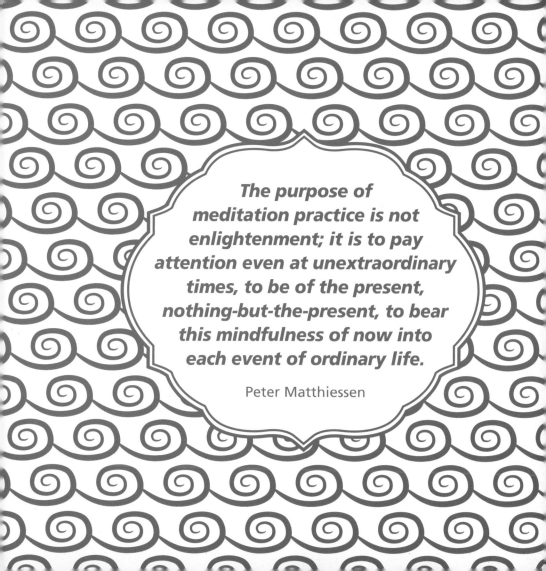

> *The purpose of meditation practice is not enlightenment; it is to pay attention even at unextraordinary times, to be of the present, nothing-but-the-present, to bear this mindfulness of now into each event of ordinary life.*
>
> Peter Matthiessen

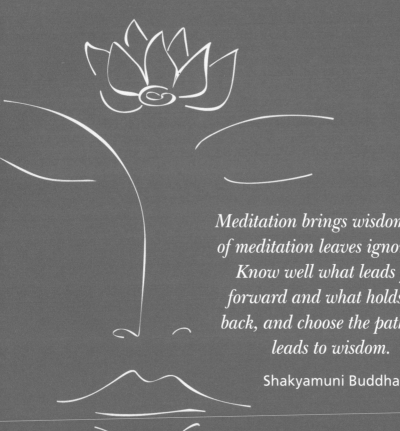

Meditation brings wisdom; lack of meditation leaves ignorance. Know well what leads you forward and what holds you back, and choose the path that leads to wisdom.

Shakyamuni Buddha

Mindfulness is not about creating a pleasant experience, but about being in the present, taking things one moment at a time and being aware of whatever arises.

> *Meditation is the tongue of the soul and the language of our spirit.*
>
> Jeremy Taylor

Tension is who you think you should be. Relaxation is who you are.

Chinese proverb

Usually, when we feel anger, we become angry. We are anger itself. When we feel depressed, we are depression. When we feel greedy, we are greed. It's easy to see ourselves in the emotional 'guise du jour' and mistake this costume for who we really are beneath it.

Marc Gilson

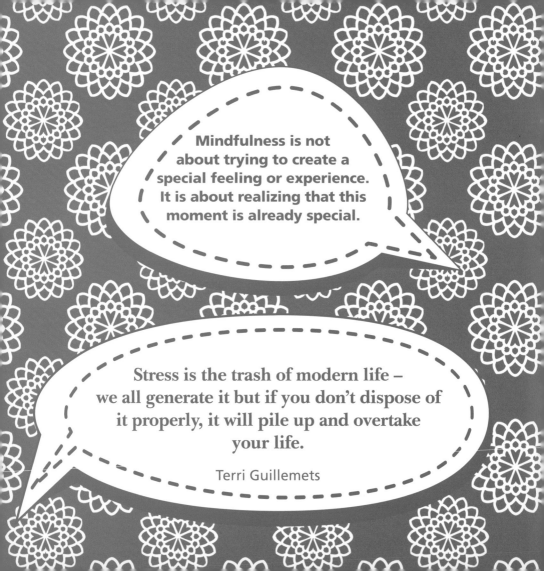

Relaxation means releasing all concern and tension and letting the natural order of life flow through one's being.

Donald Curtis

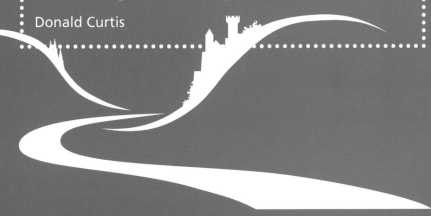

In the attitude of silence the soul finds the path in a clearer light, and what is elusive and deceptive resolves itself into crystal clearness. Our life is a long and arduous quest after Truth.

Mahatma Gandhi

The sign of intelligent people is their ability to control emotions by the application of reason.

Marya Mannes

True meditation is constant awareness, constant pliability, and clear discernment.

J. Krishnamurti

Human beings, by changing the inner attitudes of their minds, can change the outer aspects of their lives.

William James

Mindfulness isn't about trying to grasp onto this moment or forget that moment. It is about recognizing that life is made up of constantly changing moments.

One doesn't have to be religious to lead a moral life or attain wisdom.

Allan Lokos

Mindfulness is the energy that sheds light on all things and all activities, producing the power of concentration, bringing forth deep insight and awakening.

Thich Nhat Hanh

Mindfulness is hearing the music in the sound of heavy traffic.

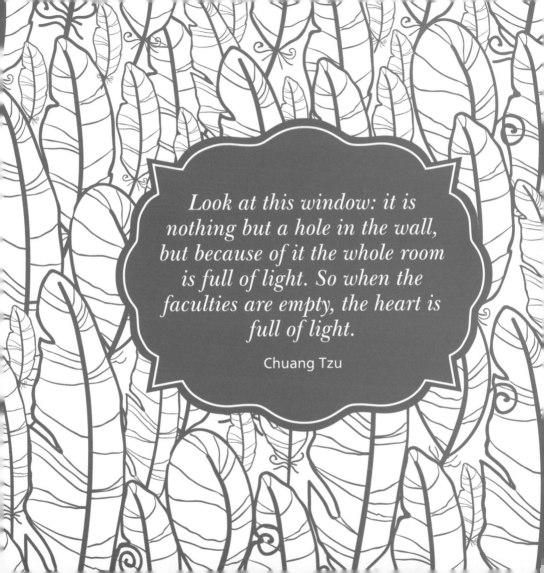

Look at this window: it is nothing but a hole in the wall, but because of it the whole room is full of light. So when the faculties are empty, the heart is full of light.

Chuang Tzu

Simplifying our lives does not mean sinking into idleness, but on the contrary, getting rid of the most subtle aspect of laziness: the one which makes us take on thousands of less important activities.

Matthieu Ricard

Meditation speaks. It speaks in silence. It reveals. It reveals to the aspirant that matter and spirit are one, quantity and quality are one, the immanent and the transcendent are one. It reveals that life can never be the mere existence of seventy or eighty years between birth and death, but is, rather, Eternity itself.

Sri Chinmoy

**Simply trust:
do not the petals flutter down,
just like that?**

Issa

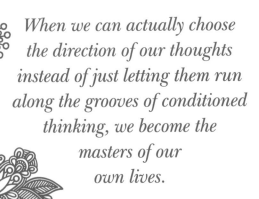

*When we can actually choose
the direction of our thoughts
instead of just letting them run
along the grooves of conditioned
thinking, we become the
masters of our
own lives.*

Eknath Easwaran

The mind in its natural state can be compared to the sky, covered by layers of cloud which hide its true nature.

Kalu Rinpoche

Do not think that what your thoughts dwell upon is of no matter. Your thoughts are making you.

Bishop Steere

Mindfulness is recognizing that we are becoming angry because we are running late, and then recognizing that we can choose instead to be calm and running late.

Mindfulness is falling awake.

Jon Kabat-Zinn

Persons of high self-esteem are not driven to make themselves superior to others; they do not seek to prove their value by measuring themselves against a comparative standard. Their joy is being who they are, not in being better than someone else.

Nathaniel Branden

EXERCISE: *Learning to be aware*

It can sometimes be hard to find the time and space to perform these exercises. You may want to get up fifteen minutes earlier than usual or set aside an agreed time each day to devote yourself to mindfulness.

1 Find a space that feels safe to you. That space can be indoors or outdoors; it just needs to feel comfortable. Turn off your mobile phone. Don't take anything with you into your 'sacred space'.

2 Close your eyes and try to relax. Listen to all the sounds you can hear. Listen to those sounds that are close by, and those that are far away. Then slowly bring your attention towards your own breathing.

3 Breathe in slowly, holding your breath for a count of five seconds once you've inhaled. Then breathe out slowly. Visualize your breath flowing out into the world. Breathe in again, slowly, visualizing the breath entering your body and filling your lungs. If you find your attention wandering, don't panic. Just recognize that your attention is wandering, and gently redirect it back towards your breathing.

4 Repeat this 'mindful breathing' for at least a minute or two. Keep practising the exercise and you will find it becomes easier. It is a powerful technique that you can use anywhere, at any time.

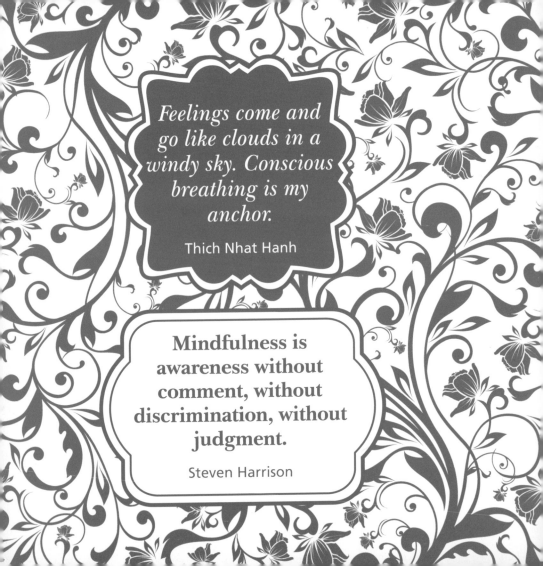

Feelings come and go like clouds in a windy sky. Conscious breathing is my anchor.

Thich Nhat Hanh

Mindfulness is awareness without comment, without discrimination, without judgment.

Steven Harrison

The greatest obstacles to inner peace are disturbing emotions such as anger, attachment, fear and suspicion, while love and compassion and a sense of universal responsibility are the sources of peace and happiness.

Dalai Lama

Awareness stems from just the right mix of concentration and relaxation.

We cannot force the development of mindfulness.

Allan Lokos

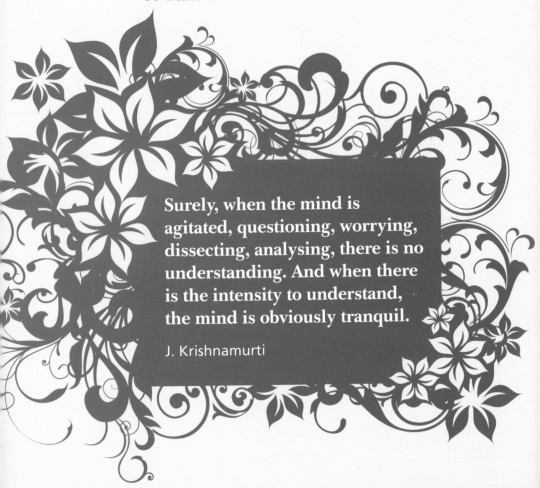

Surely, when the mind is agitated, questioning, worrying, dissecting, analysing, there is no understanding. And when there is the intensity to understand, the mind is obviously tranquil.

J. Krishnamurti

In this moment, there is plenty of time. In this moment, you are precisely as you should be. In this moment, there is infinite possibility.

Victoria Moran

A man is literally what he thinks, his character being the complete sum of all his thoughts.

James Allen

**Nowadays people are
realizing that meditation doesn't
have to be related to religion or a cult.
I think we need to change the word.**

Susie Pearl

*Who looks outside, dreams.
Who looks inside, awakens.*

C.G. Jung

Let us not look back in anger, nor forward in fear, but around in awareness.

James Thurber

Mindfulness is not simply relaxation. It takes a large amount of energy to be mindful.

Don't believe everything you think. Thoughts are just that – thoughts.

Allan Lokos

*not seeing
the room is white
until that red apple*

Anita Virgil

**Our own worst enemy
cannot harm us as much
as our unwise thoughts.
No one can help us
as much as our own
compassionate thoughts.**

Buddha

When we are mindful, deeply in touch with the present moment, our understanding of what is going on deepens, and we begin to be filled with acceptance, joy, peace and love.

Thich Nhat Hanh

Mindfulness means paying attention in a particular way: on purpose, in the present moment, and non-judgmentally.

Jon Kabat-Zinn

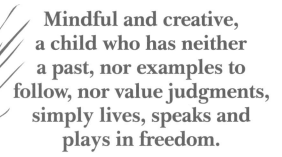

Mindful and creative,
a child who has neither
a past, nor examples to
follow, nor value judgments,
simply lives, speaks and
plays in freedom.

Arnaud Desjardins

The only way to truly discover the power of mindfulness is to learn how to do it, and then try it for yourself.

2

Becoming Who You Are

Healing may not be so much about getting better, as about letting go of everything that isn't you – all of the expectations, all of the beliefs – and becoming who you are.

Rachel Naomi Remen

Use each experience you encounter to awaken and enlighten yourself. This is the key.

Shinjo Ito

If in our daily life
we can smile, if we can be
peaceful and happy, not only we,
but everyone will profit from it.
This is the most basic kind
of peace work.

Thich Nhat Hanh

If your relationship to the present moment is not right, nothing can ever be right in the future – because when the future comes it's the present moment.

Eckhart Tolle

May my life flow like a river, ever surprised by its own unfolding.

John O'Donohue

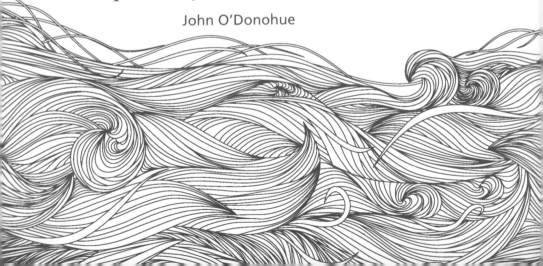

The important thing is this:
to be able at any moment to
sacrifice what we are for what
we could become.

W.E.B. DuBois

**What you do today is important,
because you are exchanging a
day of your life for it.**

Anon

*The next message you need is
always right where you are.*

Ram Dass

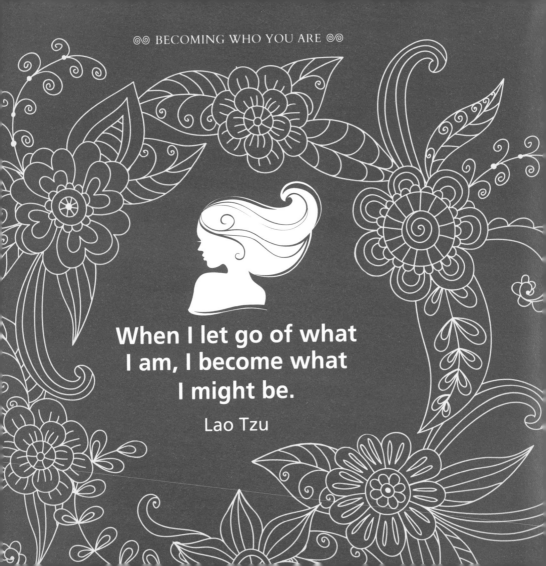

When I let go of what
I am, I become what
I might be.

Lao Tzu

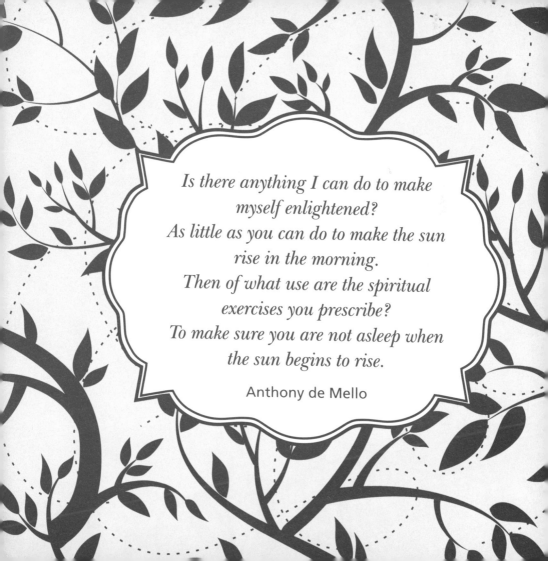

Is there anything I can do to make myself enlightened?
As little as you can do to make the sun rise in the morning.
Then of what use are the spiritual exercises you prescribe?
To make sure you are not asleep when the sun begins to rise.

Anthony de Mello

Observe the space between your thoughts, then observe the observer.

Hamilton Boudreaux

Learn to say no to demands, requests, invitations and activities that leave you with no time for yourself. Until I learned to say no, and mean it, I was always overloaded by stress.

Holly Mosier

If one is forever cautious, can one remain a human being?

Aleksandr Solzhenitsyn

Don't worry about what the world needs. Ask what makes you come alive and do that. Because what the world needs is people who have come alive.

Howard Thurman

When you set an intention, when you commit, the entire universe conspires to make it happen.

Sandy Forster

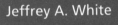

Stop, breathe, look around and embrace the miracle of each day, the miracle of life.

Jeffrey A. White

*To meditate a short time
with depth is better than
to meditate for long
hours with the mind
running wild.*

Paramhansa Yogananda

Your own
self-realization is the
greatest service you can
render the world.

Ramana Maharshi

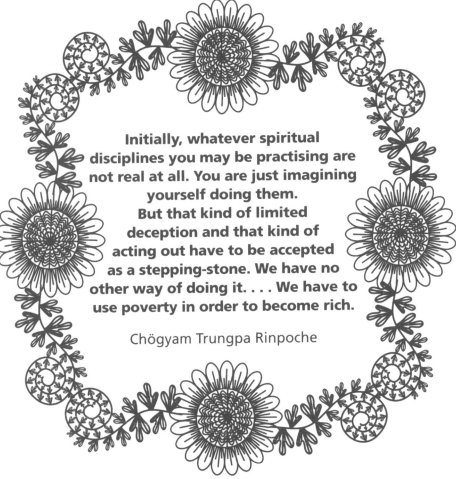

Initially, whatever spiritual disciplines you may be practising are not real at all. You are just imagining yourself doing them.
But that kind of limited deception and that kind of acting out have to be accepted as a stepping-stone. We have no other way of doing it. . . . We have to use poverty in order to become rich.

Chögyam Trungpa Rinpoche

Contemplation is a loving attainment of awareness. It is intuition of the beloved object.

Josef Pieper

Whenever you are in the head – thinking, brooding, calculating, cunning, clever – you are not total. Slowly, slowly slip out of those moments. It is just an old habit. Habits die hard. But they die certainly – if one persists, they die.

Osho

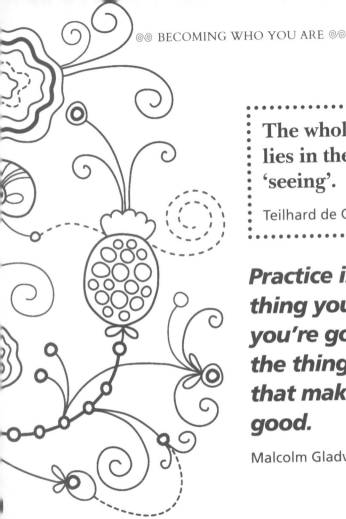

> **The whole of life lies in the verb 'seeing'.**
>
> Teilhard de Chardin

Practice isn't the thing you do once you're good. It's the thing you do that makes you good.

Malcolm Gladwell

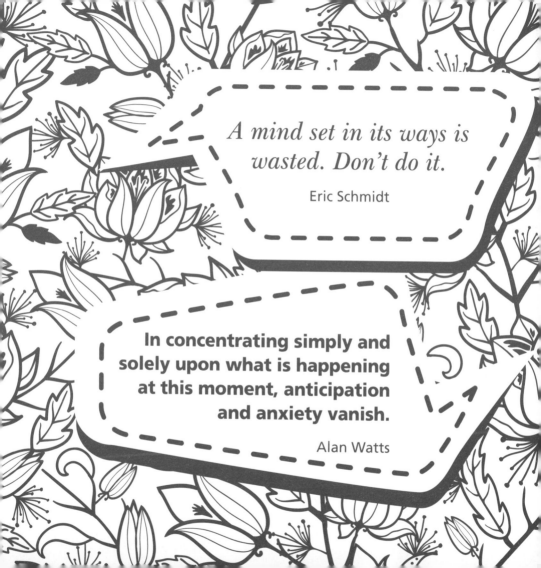

A mind set in its ways is wasted. Don't do it.

Eric Schmidt

In concentrating simply and solely upon what is happening at this moment, anticipation and anxiety vanish.

Alan Watts

Your mind is your instrument. Learn to be its master and not its slave.

Remez Sasson

Imagination will often carry us to worlds that never were, but without it we go nowhere.

Carl Sagan

The quieter you become, the more you are able to hear.

Baba Ram Dass

You should remain aware every moment of your daily life, fully conscious of what you are doing and how you are doing it.

Lama Yeshe

A good intention clothes itself with sudden power.

Ralph Waldo Emerson

Awareness is not the result of anything. There is nothing that causes it. There is nothing we can do to create it.

Steven Harrison

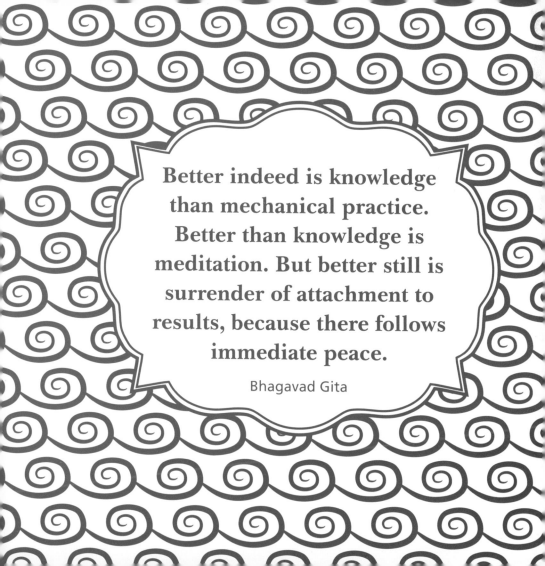

Better indeed is knowledge than mechanical practice. Better than knowledge is meditation. But better still is surrender of attachment to results, because there follows immediate peace.

Bhagavad Gita

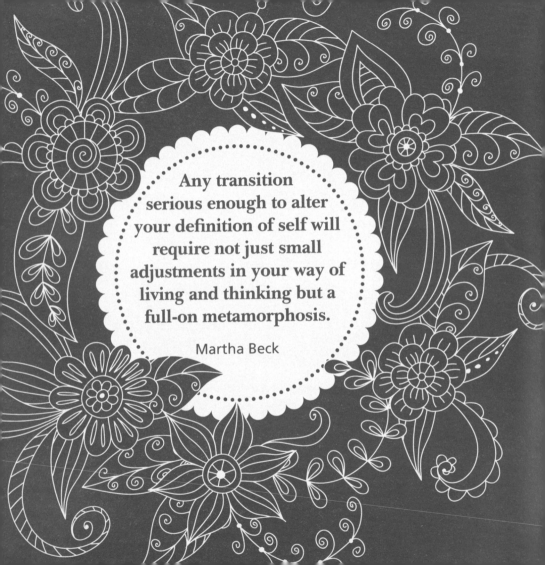

Any transition serious enough to alter your definition of self will require not just small adjustments in your way of living and thinking but a full-on metamorphosis.

Martha Beck

People only get really interesting when they start to rattle the bars of their cages.

Alain de Botton

Half of your power lies in your sameness with others. The other half lies in your uniqueness.

Alan Cohen

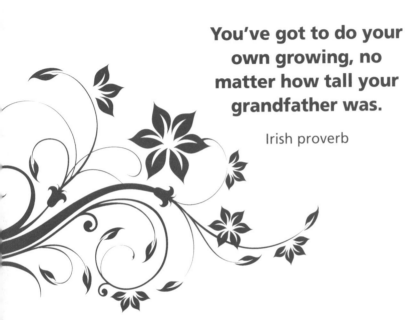

You've got to do your own growing, no matter how tall your grandfather was.

Irish proverb

In the beginning you will fall into the gaps in between thoughts – after practising for years, you become the gap.

J. Kleykamp

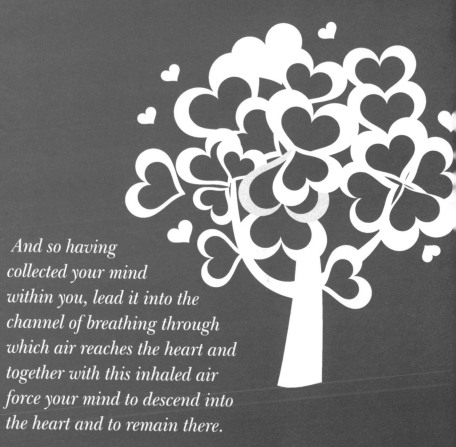

And so having collected your mind within you, lead it into the channel of breathing through which air reaches the heart and together with this inhaled air force your mind to descend into the heart and to remain there.

Nicephorus the Solitary

You cannot depend on your eyes when your imagination is out of focus.

Mark Twain

**Through concentration and meditation
you become the boss of your mind,
and gain the ability to tell it when to be
active and when to stay silent.**

Remez Sasson

*The resolved mind
hath no cares.*

George Herbert

**It is conscious intention
which confers potency in
the life of each disciple
and initiate.**

Djwhal Khul

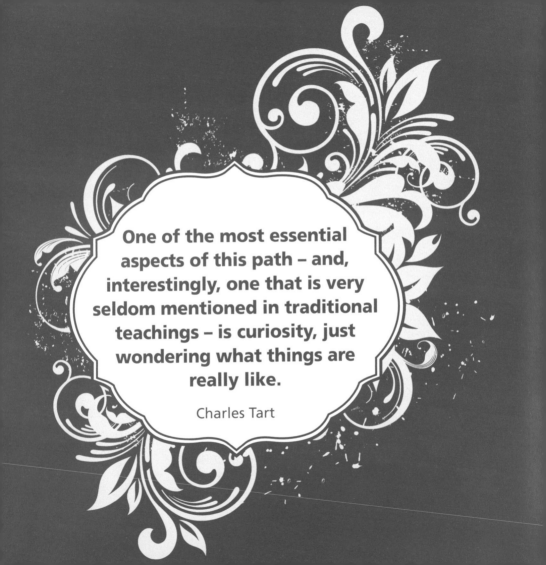

One of the most essential aspects of this path – and, interestingly, one that is very seldom mentioned in traditional teachings – is curiosity, just wondering what things are really like.

Charles Tart

The secret of happiness is freedom. The secret of freedom is courage.

Thucydides

Our intention creates our reality.

Wayne Dyer

EXERCISE: *Clouds in the sky*

This exercise is about learning who you really are, beneath all the stress and confusion. Each of us is composed of myriad thoughts and feelings, and no single one of them defines us. Many of our problems come from failing to recognize this. We get trapped in a cycle of imagined fears about the future and remembered regrets about the past.

1 Find your 'sacred space' as in the earlier exercise. Once you have relaxed, let your mind wander over recent events in your life. Recall each moment of the day, and what you were feeling or thinking at that precise time. Try to picture each of these thoughts as a cloud, moving gently across the sky.

2 You should aim to view each thought, good or bad, without judgement. Don't try to alter your thoughts. Don't criticize yourself for having them. Just recognize each thought, and observe it moving through your mind.

3 End the exercise by imagining the sky is beautiful, and cloudless. Fall in love with the present moment only, and learn to see how none of these thoughts can imprison you, as long as you realize that you are not your thoughts. Thoughts, moods and opinions come and go, like clouds across the sky.

Silence is the great teacher, and to learn its lessons you must pay attention to it. There is no substitute for the creative inspiration, knowledge, and stability that come from knowing how to contact your core of inner silence.

Deepak Chopra

Life is movement.
The more life there is,
the more flexibility there is.
The more fluid you are, the
more you are alive.

Arnaud Desjardins

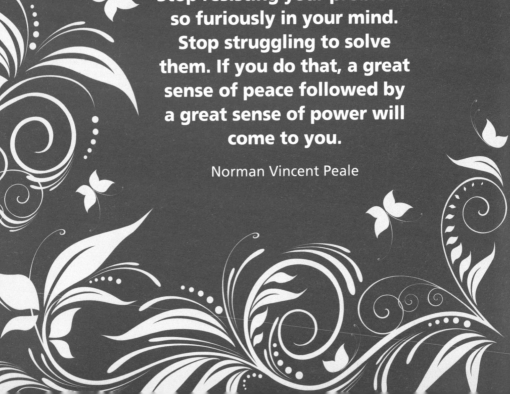

Stop resisting your problems so furiously in your mind. Stop struggling to solve them. If you do that, a great sense of peace followed by a great sense of power will come to you.

Norman Vincent Peale

Do you have patience to wait until your mud settles and the water is clear? Can you remain unmoving until the right action arises by itself?

Lao Tzu

You cannot control the results, only your actions.

Allan Lokos

The moment one definitely commits oneself, then providence moves too. All sorts of things occur to help one that would never otherwise have occurred. A whole stream of events issues from the decision, raising in one's favour all manner of unforeseen incidents, meetings and material assistance which no man could have dreamed would have come his way.

W.H. Murray

Set peace of mind as your highest goal, and organize your life around it.

Brian Tracy

To observe 'what is', the mind must be free of all comparison of the ideal, of the opposite. Then you will see what actually 'is' is far more important than what 'should be'.

J. Krishnamurti

You have to remember one life, one death – this one! To enter fully the day, the hour, the moment whether it appears as life or death, whether we catch it on the inbreath or outbreath, requires only a moment – this moment.

Stephen Levine

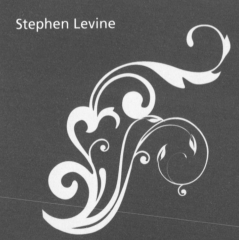

Cherish that which is within you.

Chuang Tzu

It takes a deep commitment to change
and an even deeper commitment to grow.

Ralph Ellison

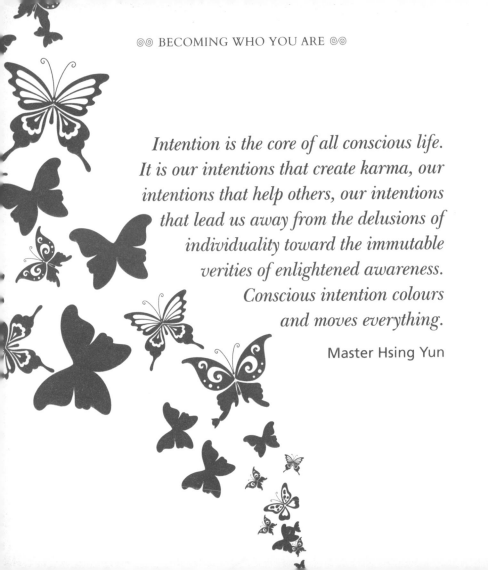

*Intention is the core of all conscious life.
It is our intentions that create karma, our
intentions that help others, our intentions
that lead us away from the delusions of
individuality toward the immutable
verities of enlightened awareness.
Conscious intention colours
and moves everything.*

Master Hsing Yun

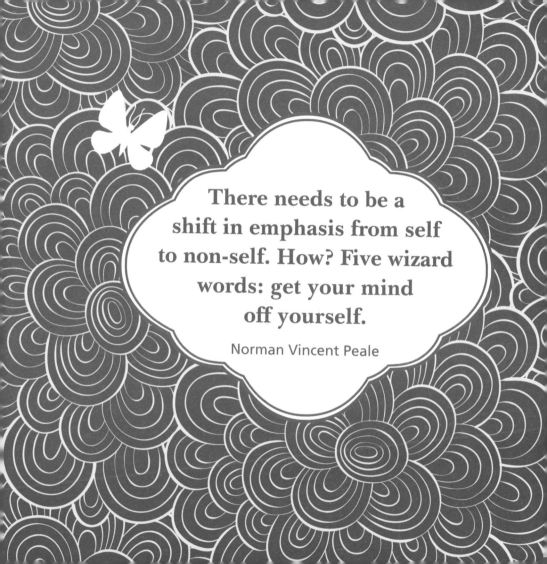

There needs to be a shift in emphasis from self to non-self. How? Five wizard words: get your mind off yourself.

Norman Vincent Peale

As you practise choiceless awareness, simply observe what's predominant or compelling in the mind and body and be present to it. If nothing is especially prevalent and you're unsure of where to place your attention, you can always go back to the breath, sensations, sounds, or thoughts and emotions as a way to anchor into the here and now.

Bob Stahl

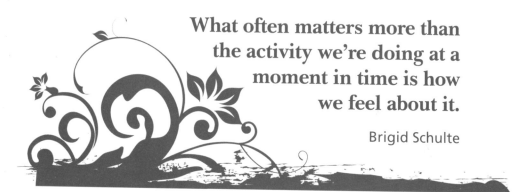

What often matters more than the activity we're doing at a moment in time is how we feel about it.

Brigid Schulte

Commitment doesn't mean that it has to last forever, but while you are there, commit yourself 100 per cent. By doing this, the quality of your life improves 100 per cent.

Susan Jeffers

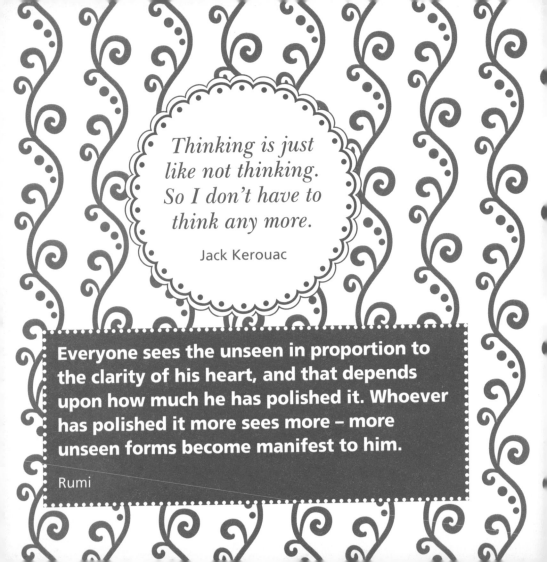

Thinking is just like not thinking. So I don't have to think any more.

Jack Kerouac

Everyone sees the unseen in proportion to the clarity of his heart, and that depends upon how much he has polished it. Whoever has polished it more sees more – more unseen forms become manifest to him.

Rumi

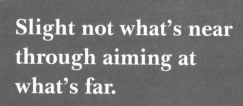

Slight not what's near
through aiming at
what's far.

Euripides

*Those who do not have power over
the story that dominates their lives,
the power to retell it, rethink it,
deconstruct it, joke about it, and
change it as times change, truly are
powerless, because they cannot think
new thoughts.*

Salman Rushdie

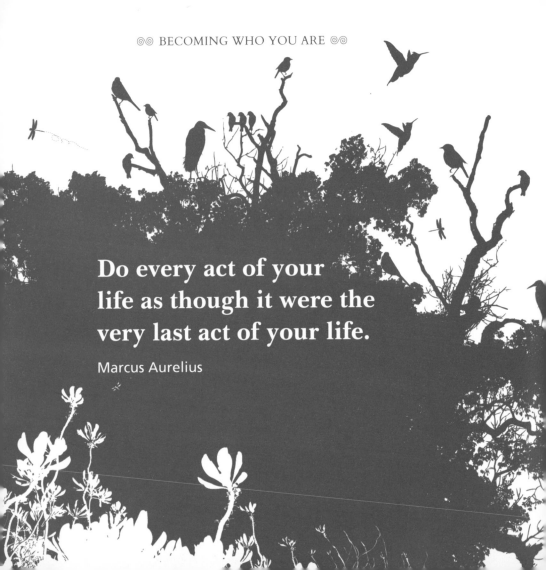

Do every act of your life as though it were the very last act of your life.

Marcus Aurelius

*Commitment is what transforms
a promise into reality.*

**Restore your attention or bring it to
a new level by dramatically slowing
down whatever you're doing.**

Sharon Salzberg

*Softly and kindly
remind yourself,
'I cannot own
anything.'*

Wayne Dyer

**No destination
Is reached by clouds
   in the sky
Only endless change**

Marc Hoy

Be here now.

Ram Dass

The most fundamental aggression to ourselves, the most fundamental harm we can do to ourselves, is to remain ignorant by not having the courage and the respect to look at ourselves honestly and gently.

Pema Chödrön

We are all sculptors and painters, and our material is our own flesh and blood and bones. Any nobleness begins at once to refine a man's features, any meanness or sensuality to imbrute them.

Henry David Thoreau

Concentrate all your thoughts on the task at hand. The sun's rays do not burn until brought into focus.

Alexander Graham Bell

Life is all memory,
except for the one
present moment that
goes by you so quickly
you hardly catch
it going.

Tennessee Williams

What you get by achieving your goals is not as important as what you become by achieving your goals.

Henry David Thoreau

Sit still, be silent, let composure creep over you.

Norman Vincent Peale

Non-doing simply means letting things be and allowing them to unfold in their own way. Enormous effort can be involved, but it is a graceful, knowledgeable, effortless effort, a doerless doing.

Jon Kabat-Zinn

Looking at beauty in the world is the first step of purifying the mind.

Amit Ray

There's only one reason why you're not experiencing bliss at this present moment, and it's because you're thinking or focusing on what you don't have. . . . But, right now you have everything you need to be in bliss.

Anthony de Mello

Respond; don't react.
Listen; don't talk.
Think; don't assume.

Raji Lukkoor

No technique, no communication skill or psychological process can come anywhere close to the effectiveness of being 100 per cent present. It is not an easy thing to do.

Danaan Parry

The present moment is filled with joy and happiness. If you are attentive, you will see it.

Thich Nhat Hanh

*Losing its name
a river
enters the sea*

John Sandbach

A small key opens big doors.

Turkish proverb

The practice of mindfulness begins in the small, remote cave of your unconscious mind and blossoms with the sunlight of your conscious life, reaching far beyond the people and places you can see.

Earon Davis

You shouldn't run away from your problems, you need to aim straight for the heart of the beast.

Ruby Wax

When we meditate on the body-mind process, the 'noting mind' or 'observing mind' will choose the object itself.

Chanmyay Sayadaw U Janakabhivamsa

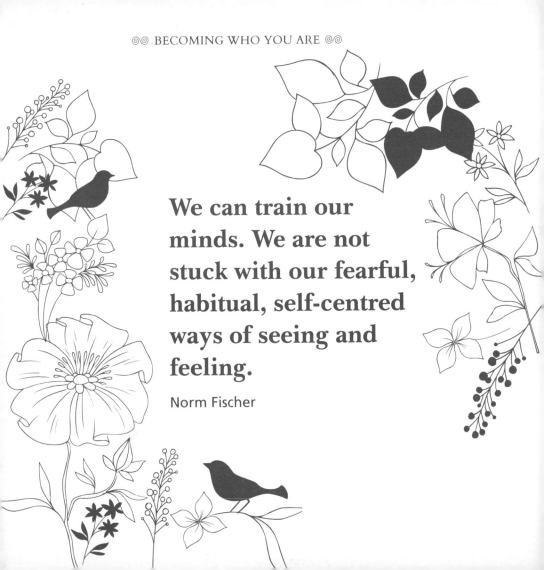

We can train our minds. We are not stuck with our fearful, habitual, self-centred ways of seeing and feeling.

Norm Fischer

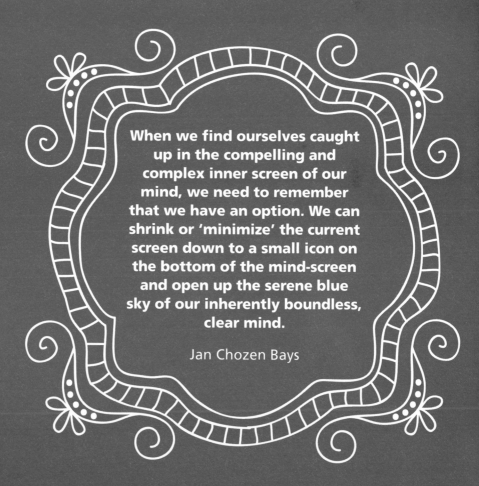

When we find ourselves caught up in the compelling and complex inner screen of our mind, we need to remember that we have an option. We can shrink or 'minimize' the current screen down to a small icon on the bottom of the mind-screen and open up the serene blue sky of our inherently boundless, clear mind.

Jan Chozen Bays

We can learn a lot from children. We need to take more time to be playful and enjoy simple things.

Jayne Morris

Paying attention to and staying with finer and finer sensations within the body is one of the surest ways to steady the wandering mind.

Ravi Ravindra

Step into mindfulness with particular attention to what is being said. As you listen, mindfulness is alert with a question something like, 'What is happening now?'

Gregory Kramer

How do you let go?
You just let go.

Vernon Howard

Why should we observe or watch physical and mental processes as they are? Because we want to realize their true nature.

Chanmyay Sayadaw U Janakabhivamsa

If you concentrate on finding whatever is good in every situation, you will discover that your life will suddenly be filled with gratitude, a feeling that nurtures the soul.

Rabbi Harold Kushner

I keep looking for one more teacher, only to find that fish learn from the water and birds learn from the sky.

Mark Nepo

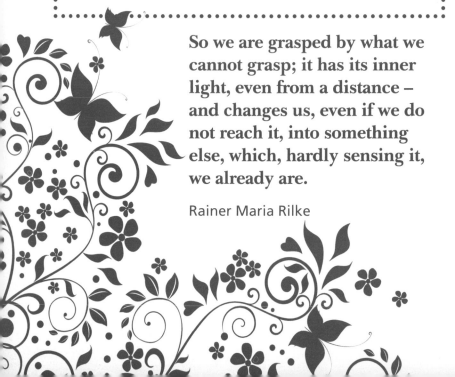

So we are grasped by what we cannot grasp; it has its inner light, even from a distance – and changes us, even if we do not reach it, into something else, which, hardly sensing it, we already are.

Rainer Maria Rilke

Everyday
Mindfulness

In mindfulness one is
not only restful and happy,
but alert and awake. Meditation
is not evasion, it is a serene
encounter with reality.

Thich Nhat Hanh

Knowledge is learning something every day. Wisdom is letting go of something every day.

Zen proverb

Mindfulness isn't difficult, we just need to remember to do it.

Sharon Salzberg

Life is a process of becoming, a combination of states we have to go through. Where people fail is that they wish to elect a state and remain in it. This is a kind of death.

Anaïs Nin

*How many things
I can do without!*

Socrates

For most of us, a
typical day involves hurrying
from task to task, forgetting that there
are other possibilities for us. Even a tiny bit of
mindfulness, brought to any moment, can wake
us up, thus subverting the momentum of
doing for at least one moment.

Mark Williams

In seed time learn,
in harvest teach, in
winter enjoy.

William Blake

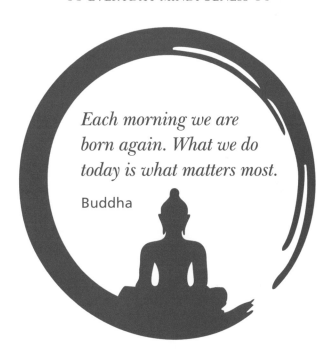

Each morning we are born again. What we do today is what matters most.

Buddha

Miracles rest not so much upon faces or voices or healing power coming to us from far off, but on our perceptions being made finer, so that for a moment our eyes can see and our ears can hear what is there about us always.

Willa Cather

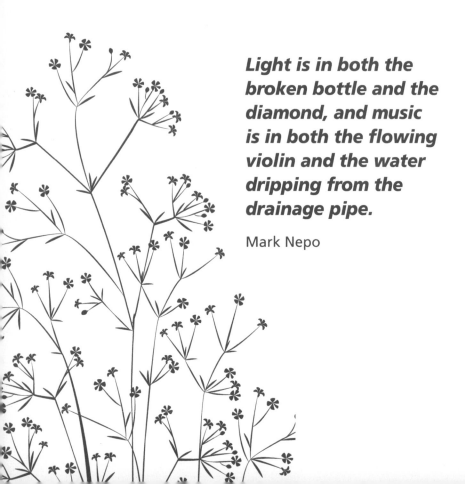

Light is in both the broken bottle and the diamond, and music is in both the flowing violin and the water dripping from the drainage pipe.

Mark Nepo

When even one virtue becomes our nature, the mind becomes clean and tranquil. Then there is no need to practise meditation; we will automatically be meditating always.

Swami Satchidananda

Every moment there is a possibility to be total. Whatsoever you are doing, be absorbed in it so utterly that the mind thinks nothing, is just there, is just a presence.

Osho

Always hold fast to the present. Every situation, indeed every moment, is of infinite value, for it is the representative of a whole eternity.

Johann Wolfgang von Goethe

No matter how much pressure you feel at work, if you could find ways to relax for at least five minutes every hour, you'd be more productive.

Dr Joyce Brothers

Our repeated failure to fully act as we would wish must not discourage us. It is the sincere intention that is the essential thing, and this will in time release us from the bondage of habits which at present seem almost insurmountable.

Thomas Troward

We do not remember days, we remember moments.

Cesare Pavese

We can judge our progress by the courage of our questions and the depth of our answers, our willingness to embrace what is true rather than what feels good.

Carl Sagan

The hustle and bustle of everyday life desensitizes us from the universe. Mindfulness helps to resensitize us to the wonders of our lives.

Few of us ever live in the present. We are forever anticipating what is to come or remembering what has gone.

Louis L'Amour

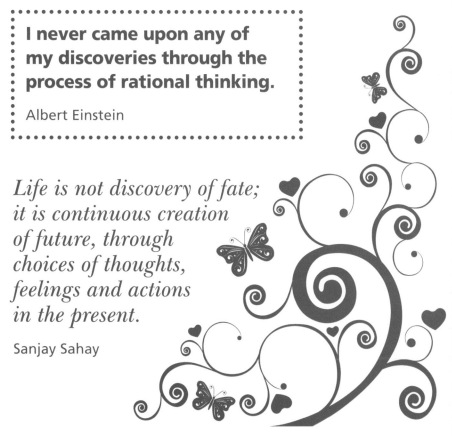

I never came upon any of my discoveries through the process of rational thinking.

Albert Einstein

Life is not discovery of fate; it is continuous creation of future, through choices of thoughts, feelings and actions in the present.

Sanjay Sahay

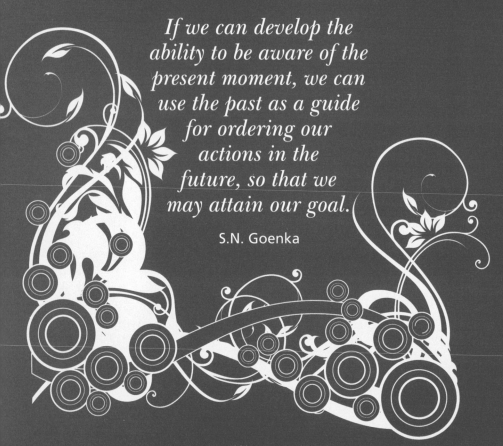

*If we can develop the
ability to be aware of the
present moment, we can
use the past as a guide
for ordering our
actions in the
future, so that we
may attain our goal.*

S.N. Goenka

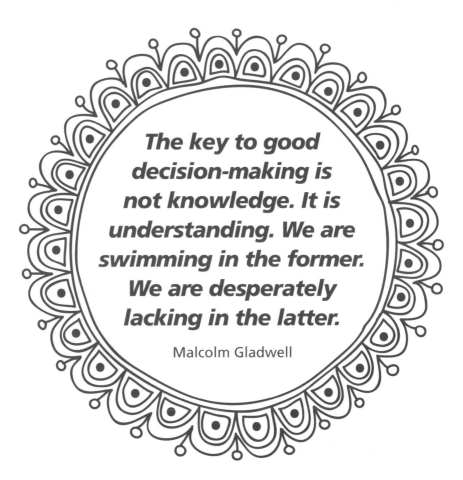

The key to good decision-making is not knowledge. It is understanding. We are swimming in the former. We are desperately lacking in the latter.

Malcolm Gladwell

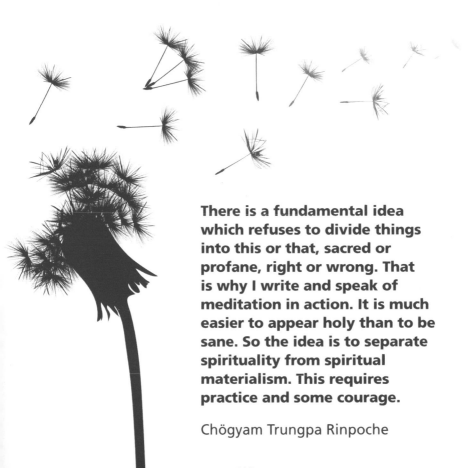

There is a fundamental idea which refuses to divide things into this or that, sacred or profane, right or wrong. That is why I write and speak of meditation in action. It is much easier to appear holy than to be sane. So the idea is to separate spirituality from spiritual materialism. This requires practice and some courage.

Chögyam Trungpa Rinpoche

A man or woman becomes fully human only by his or her choices and his or her commitment to them. People attain worth and dignity by the multitude of decisions they make from day to day. These decisions require courage.

Rollo May

We must be willing to let go of the life we have planned, so as to accept the life that is waiting for us.

Joseph Campbell

**Inspiration
is intention
obeyed.**

Emily Carr

*Until one is committed,
there is hesitancy, the
chance to draw back,
always ineffectiveness.*

W.H. Murray

**Wanderer, your footsteps are
the road, and nothing more;
wanderer, there is no road,
the road is made by walking.**

Antonio Machado

No age is too early or too late for the health of the soul.

Epicurus

Mindfulness helps to smooth out all the ups and downs of our daily lives.

Power is the capacity to translate intention into reality and then sustain it.

Warren Bennis

If you can find as much happiness at the bottom of the ladder of success as you can at the top, then you understand contentment.

Tom Krause

The beginning of wisdom is found in doubting; by doubting we come to the question.

Pierre Abela

The range of what we think and do is limited by what we fail to notice. And because we fail to notice that we fail to notice there is nothing we can do to change until we notice how failing to notice shapes our thoughts and deeds.

R.D. Laing

Man's mind, once stretched by a new idea, never regains its original dimension.

Oliver Wendell Holmes

It's the company, not the cooking, that makes a meal.

Kirby Larson

Living in the moment means letting go of the past and not waiting for the future. It means living your life consciously, aware that each moment you breathe is a gift.

Oprah Winfrey

It is not enough to stare up the steps; we must step up the stairs.

Vaclav Havel

Do not wait to strike till the iron is hot; but make it hot by striking.

William B. Sprague

What you are today is a consequence of what you were yesterday. What you will be tomorrow will be the consequence of what you are today.

The easiest thing in the world is self-deceit; for every man believes what he wishes, though the reality is often different.

Demosthenes

You might be tempted to avoid the messiness of daily living for the tranquillity of stillness and peacefulness. This of course would be an attachment to stillness, and like any strong attachment, it leads to delusion. It arrests development and short-circuits the cultivation of wisdom.

Jon Kabat-Zinn

Every breath is an opportunity to receive and let go. I receive love and I let go of pain.

Brenda MacIntyre

Mindfulness sharpens your concentration, which means that not only are you likely to be calmer at work, you're also likely to be more productive.

If we do not find anything pleasant, at least we shall find something new.

Voltaire

This isn't just 'another day, another dollar'. It's more like 'another day, another miracle'.

Victoria Moran

There is a difference between interest and commitment. When you're interested in something, you do it only when it's convenient. When you're committed to something, you accept no excuses, only results.

Ken Blanchard

Confidence on the outside begins by living with integrity on the inside.

Brian Tracy

It is not the strongest of the species that survive, nor the most intelligent, but the one most responsive to change.

Charles Darwin

> *Education's purpose is to replace an empty mind with an open one.*
>
> Malcolm Forbes

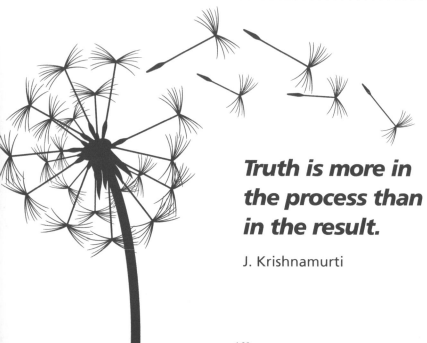

Truth is more in the process than in the result.

J. Krishnamurti

It doesn't matter how slowly you go as long as you don't stop.

Confucius

Concentrate not on the results, but on the value, the rightness, the truth of the work itself.

Thomas Merton

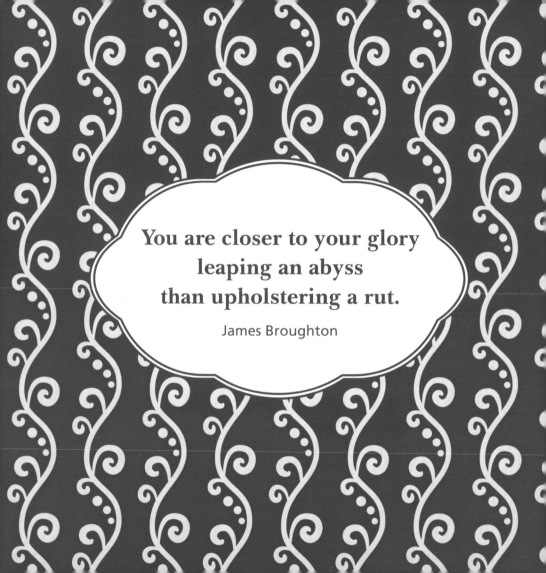

You are closer to your glory
leaping an abyss
than upholstering a rut.

James Broughton

In silence there is eloquence. Stop weaving and watch how the pattern improves.

Rumi

Work, sex, and money are actually the energy outlet of society, its energy radiation, the expression of its sacredness. So we should try to see the spiritual implications of society, the spirituality even within Madison Avenue or Wall Street.

Chögyam Trungpa Rinpoche

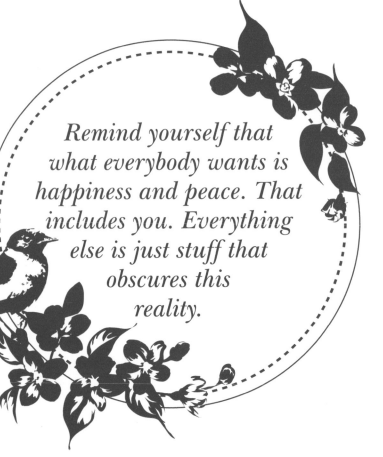

Remind yourself that what everybody wants is happiness and peace. That includes you. Everything else is just stuff that obscures this reality.

Everything is created twice, first in the mind and then in reality.

Robin S. Sharma

Western laziness consists of cramming our lives with compulsive activity, so that there is no time at all to confront the real issues.

Sogyal Rinpoche

The eyes see only what the mind is prepared to comprehend.

Henri Louis Bergson

One is a great deal less anxious if one feels perfectly free to be anxious, and the same may be said of guilt.

The purpose of a life is a life of purpose.

Robert Byrne

The doors we open and close each day decide the lives we live.

Flora Whittemore

The wren
Earns his living
Noiselessly.

Issa

Keep on beginning and failing. Each time you fail, start all over again, and you will grow stronger until you have accomplished a purpose – not the one you began with, perhaps, but one you'll be glad to remember.

Anne Sullivan

If you wait for tomorrow, tomorrow comes. If you don't wait for tomorrow, tomorrow comes.

Senegalese proverb

True happiness, we are told, consists in getting out of oneself; but the point is not only to get out – you must stay out; and to stay out you must have some absorbing errand.

Henry James

> ***Without giving up hope – that there's somewhere better to be, that there's someone better to be – we will never relax with where we are or who we are.***
>
> Pema Chödrön

Don't let a day go by without asking who you are.

Deepak Chopra

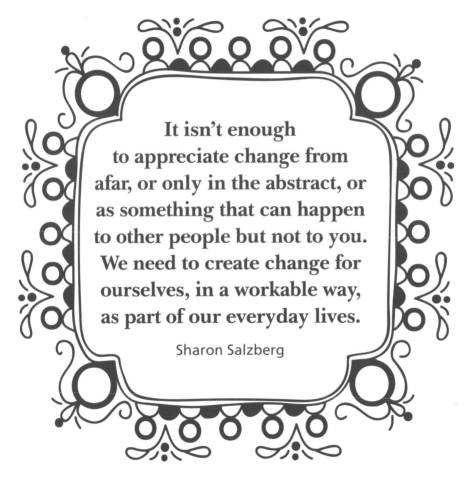

It isn't enough
to appreciate change from
afar, or only in the abstract, or
as something that can happen
to other people but not to you.
We need to create change for
ourselves, in a workable way,
as part of our everyday lives.

Sharon Salzberg

While we're talking, envious time is fleeing: seize the day, put no trust in the future.

Horace

Stop allowing your day-to-day life to be clouded by busy nothingness.

Steve Maraboli

Everything is a miracle. It is a miracle that one does not dissolve in one's bath like a lump of sugar.

Pablo Picasso

Don't try to rush things: for the cup to run over, it must first be filled.

Antonio Machado

Insight is not a light bulb that goes off inside our heads. It is a flickering candle that can easily be snuffed out.

Malcolm Gladwell

Enlightenment is the result of the daily practice of mindfulness.

Shinjo Ito

Patience may seem like a superficial virtue, but actually it embodies a deep insight into the nature of things: they're intertwining, messy, imperfectible, and usually not about you.

Rick Hanson

Hiding how much of a mess you feel is exhausting. Recognize when you are doing this, and channel that energy into being mindful of your problems instead.

Patience has all the time it needs.

Allan Lokos

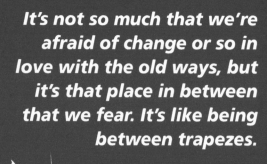

It's not so much that we're afraid of change or so in love with the old ways, but it's that place in between that we fear. It's like being between trapezes.

Marilyn Ferguson

A man's character is his fate.

Heraclitus

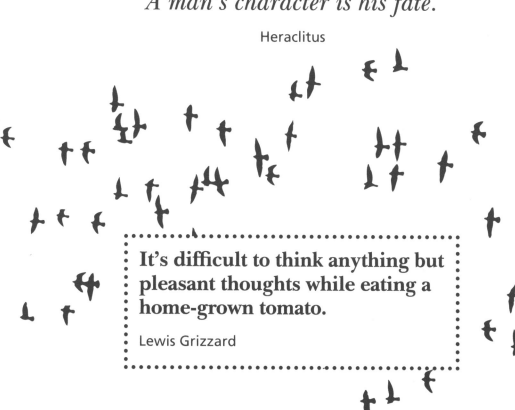

It's difficult to think anything but pleasant thoughts while eating a home-grown tomato.

Lewis Grizzard

EXERCISE: *The wonder of the everyday*

This exercise is designed to reconnect you with the beauty of the natural world. It is so easy to get lost in the hustle and bustle of everyday life, and miss much of nature's wonder.

1 Choose some part of the natural world to focus your attention on. It could be the sky, or the moon, or it could be something much smaller, such as a flower, or even a weed between paving stones.

2 Imagine that your attention is a ball of light. Gradually narrow that ball of light until it is a single beam, focused entirely on the object you have selected. Breathing gently, just observe that object, as if you were noticing it for the first time. Imagine it has suddenly emerged into your consciousness and was never really there before. Notice any movements, or changes in colour or texture. Let yourself become aware of its myriad facets.

3 Observe how this small part of the universe 'just is', without worrying over whether it should be, or deserves to be. Once you are truly mindful of the world, you begin to realize that everything in the world is in the right place – including you.

People attain worth and dignity by the multitude of decisions they make from day to day.

Rollo May

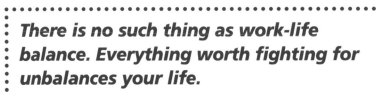

> *There is no such thing as work-life balance. Everything worth fighting for unbalances your life.*
>
> Alain de Botton

To slave away on the pointless business of mundane life, and then to come out empty – it is a tragic error.

Tibetan Book of the Dead

When eating fruit, remember who planted the tree; when drinking water, remember who dug the well.

Vietnamese proverb

The truth may be puzzling . . .
It may be counter-intuitive. It may
contradict deeply held prejudices.
It may not be consonant with
what we desperately want to be
true. But our preferences do not
determine what's true.

Carl Sagan

The doors of wisdom are never shut.

Benjamin Franklin

Distracting yourself away from your problems doesn't help you: problems will always return. Acknowledging your problems is the first step to dealing with them.

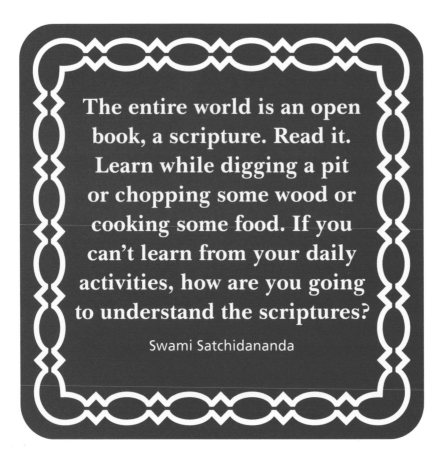

The entire world is an open book, a scripture. Read it. Learn while digging a pit or chopping some wood or cooking some food. If you can't learn from your daily activities, how are you going to understand the scriptures?

Swami Satchidananda

Silence is that which has been going on while there was talking.

J. Krishnamurti

The solution to our mood problems may not require heroic attempts to change our inner feeling world or the outer world of people, places, and jobs. Rather, it may simply involve a shift in the way we pay attention to all of them.

Mark Williams

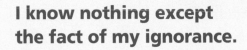

I know nothing except the fact of my ignorance.

Socrates

The little things we do in life may not seem to have a direct bearing on spirituality; maybe they seem quite unspiritual. Nevertheless, it is your world you are dealing with; it is your environment. So the things you are doing should be felt fully rather than rushed through.

Chögyam Trungpa Rinpoche

As you walk and eat and travel, be where you are. Otherwise you will miss most of your life.

Buddha

**Try dying every day
to your old self . . .
So that you emerge
renewed and
young again as the
tired mind sheds
its load.**

Kristin Zambucka

*Before enlightenment, chop wood,
carry water. After enlightenment,
chop wood, carry water.*

Zen proverb

4

Mindful
Relationships

Love is more than just a feeling. It's a process requiring continual attention. Loving well takes laughter, loyalty, and wanting more to be able to say 'I understand' than to hear 'You're right'.

Molleen Matsumura

Most people have a harder time letting themselves love than finding someone to love them.

Bill Russell

Ultimately, it is only by mindfully caring for ourselves that we can truly and effectively care for others with compassion.

Arnie Kozak

The act of compassion
begins with full attention,
just as rapport does. You have
to really see the person. If you
see the person, then naturally,
empathy arises. If you tune into
the other person, you feel with
them . . . You want to help them,
and then that begins a
compassionate act.

Daniel Goleman

Love does not obey our expectations, it obeys our intentions.

Lloyd Strom

True compassion is undirected and holds no conceptual focus. That kind of genuine, true compassion is only possible after realizing emptiness.

Tsoknyi Rinpoche

One rarely falls in love without being as much attracted to what is interestingly wrong with someone as what is objectively healthy.

Alain de Botton

Hanging onto resentment is letting someone you despise live rent-free in your head.

Ann Landers

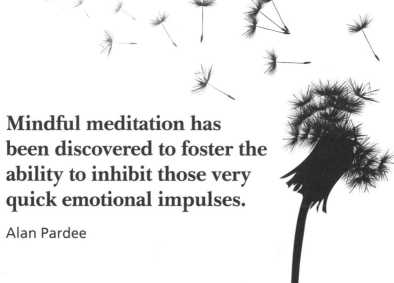

Mindful meditation has been discovered to foster the ability to inhibit those very quick emotional impulses.

Alan Pardee

Men do not attract that which they want, but that which they are.

James Allen

Harm in the name of help is one of the oldest games. The grand inquisitor of the Spanish Inquisition spouted the loftiest of motives. The Salem witchcraft trials were conducted for the 'public good'.

Bhante Henepola Gunaratana

To develop this mind state of compassion is to learn to live, as the Buddha put it, with sympathy for all living beings, without exception.

Sharon Salzberg

No snowflake in an avalanche ever feels responsible.

Voltaire

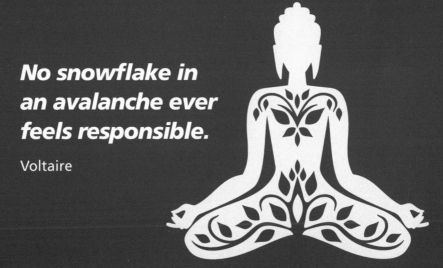

As long as we have practised neither concentration nor mindfulness, the ego takes itself for granted and remains its usual normal size, as big as the people around one will allow.

Ayya Khema

Youth fades; love droops; the leaves of friendship fall. A mother's secret hope outlives them all.

Oliver Wendell Holmes

The individual is capable of both great compassion and great indifference. He has it within his means to nourish the former and outgrow the latter.

Norman Cousins

The moment we cease to hold each other, the sea engulfs us and the light goes out.

James Baldwin

Be patient toward all that is unsolved in your heart and try to love the questions themselves, like locked rooms and like books that are now written in a very foreign tongue.

Rainer Maria Rilke

Let the beauty we love be what we do.

Rumi

All beings want to be happy, yet so very few know how. It is out of ignorance that any of us cause suffering, for ourselves or for others.

Sharon Salzberg

If I dare to hear you, I will feel you like the sun, and grow in your direction.

Mark Nepo

If someone comes along and shoots an arrow into your heart, it's fruitless to stand there and yell at the person. It would be much better to turn your attention to the fact that there's an arrow in your heart.

Pema Chödrön

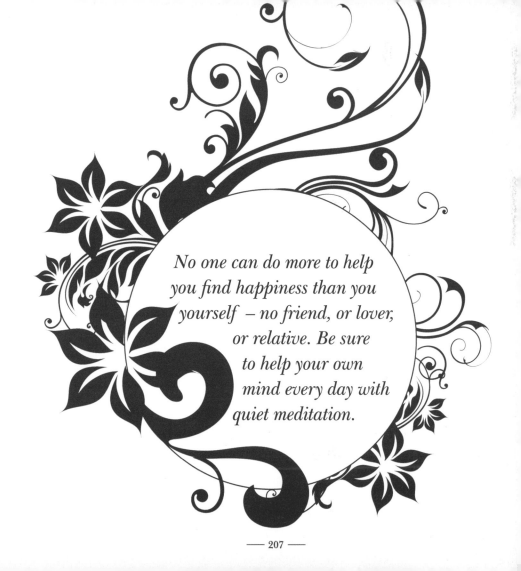

No one can do more to help you find happiness than you yourself – no friend, or lover, or relative. Be sure to help your own mind every day with quiet meditation.

One person's awakening will enlighten countless others.

Shinjo Ito

In the end, just three things matter: how well we have lived, how well we have loved, how well we have learned to let go.

Jack Kornfield

Dining with one's friends and beloved family is certainly one of life's primal and most innocent delights, one that is both soul-satisfying and eternal.

Julia Child

Love is more than a noun
– it is a verb; it is more
than a feeling – it
is caring, sharing,
helping, sacrificing.

William Arthur Ward

Do not speak about anyone who is not physically present.

Allan Lokos

Festivals show that people are desperate – to let go, play, connect with others and ultimately have fun.

Claire Hamilton

I suffer from 'Room B' syndrome. I always think other people are having a better time than me. Social media has made this worse – when comparing yourself to others, you rarely come out favourably.

Cherry Healey

*There's no such thing as a bad
emotion, only an unprocessed one.*

Rachel Naomi Remen

**If we could read the secret history of our enemies,
we should find in each man's life sorrow and
suffering enough to disarm all hostility.**

Henry Wadsworth Longfellow

Change will only come about when each of us takes up the daily struggle ourselves to be more forgiving, compassionate, loving, and above all joyful in the knowledge that, by some miracle of grace, we can change as those around us can change, too.

Mairead Maguire

Through meditation, we become aware of ourselves exactly as we are, by waking up to the numerous subtle ways that we act out our own selfishness. Then we truly begin to be genuinely selfless. Cleansing yourself of selfishness is not a selfish activity.

Bhante Henepola Gunaratana

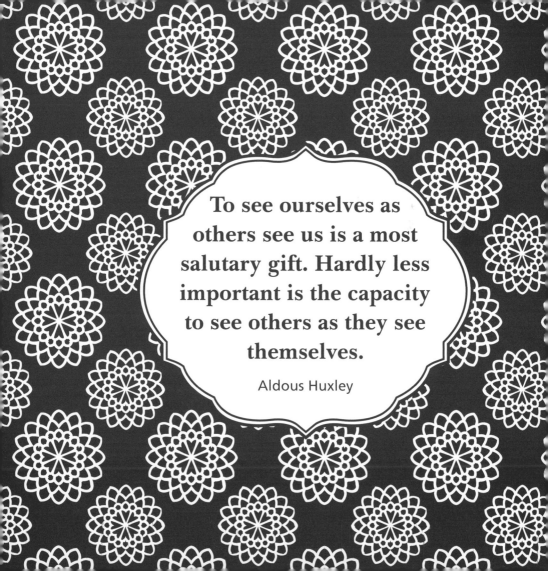

To see ourselves as others see us is a most salutary gift. Hardly less important is the capacity to see others as they see themselves.

Aldous Huxley

Patience also contains a wonderful teaching about desire: wish for something, sure, but be at peace when you can't have it. Patience knows you can't make the river flow any faster.

Rick Hanson

The moment you follow someone you cease to follow Truth.

J. Krishnamurti

Love comes from understanding others. And to understand others we must first understand ourselves.

Anger is a short madness.

Horace

The more you involve yourself with society, the more experiences you have, the more workable situations will become. The intensity of your engagement brings space.

Chögyam Trungpa Rinpoche

We can bring our spiritual practice into the streets, into our communities, when we see each realm as a temple, as a place to discover that which is sacred.

Jack Kornfield

The only lasting beauty is the beauty of the heart.

Rumi

We need, in love, to practise only this: letting each other go. For holding on comes easily; we do not need to learn it.

Rainer Maria Rilke

Let us be grateful to people who make us happy; they are the charming gardeners who make our souls blossom.

Marcel Proust

Friendship is a single soul dwelling in two bodies.

Aristotle

The direct use of force is such a poor solution to any problem, it is generally employed only by small children and large nations.

David Friedman

Like trying to cut wood with a dull axe, trying to take care of others without taking care of the self first is a counterproductive strategy.

Arnie Kozak

Treat everyone you meet as if they were you.

Doug Dillon

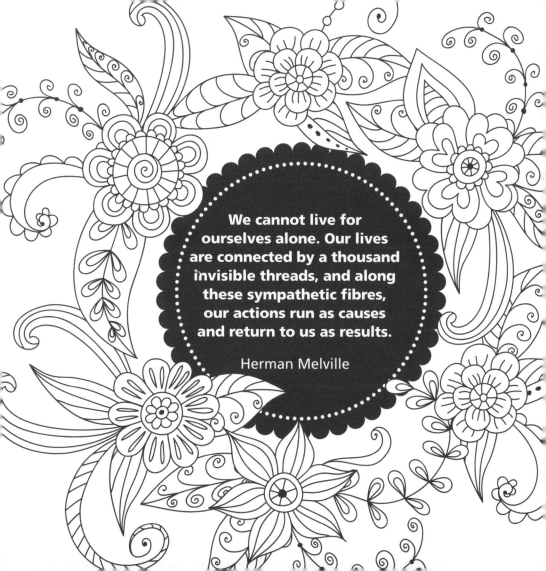

We cannot live for ourselves alone. Our lives are connected by a thousand invisible threads, and along these sympathetic fibres, our actions run as causes and return to us as results.

Herman Melville

EXERCISE: *Mindful listening*

This exercise is designed to help you become more aware of the subconscious habits that tend to creep into everyday conversations. By becoming mindful of these habits we can begin to change them if we feel they are getting in the way of true communication.

1 Listen in on a conversation, either between strangers or between colleagues or friends. You may choose to do this at work, or on the bus – or you can even do it by listening to a radio or television programme, if you're uncomfortable overhearing people in public. Pay close attention to what each speaker in the conversation is saying. Focus on the words themselves, and also upon the intonation, and any body language that accompanies it.

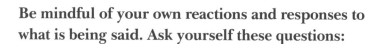

Be mindful of your own reactions and responses to what is being said. Ask yourself these questions:

2 Do I feel the urge to join in by sharing an experience I have had? If so, why? Is it because I believe the experience is related, or interesting, or impressive? Is it because I believe the person would be helped by hearing my experience, or is it because it would help me to share it? Or perhaps it is because I think sharing the story would make them like me?

3 Do I feel the urge to offer advice?

4 Am I making any assumptions about the people having the conversation?

5 Are any of the things being said causing me to feel anger, or frustration? If so, what are the triggers for this?

Under the present brutal and primitive conditions on this planet, every person you meet should be regarded as one of the walking wounded.

Robert Anton Wilson

People, even more than things, have to be restored, renewed, revived, reclaimed, and redeemed. Never throw out anyone.

Audrey Hepburn

Let go of your attachment to being right, and suddenly your mind is more open. You're able to benefit from the unique viewpoints of others, without being crippled by your own judgment.

Ralph Marston

> *We have two ears and one mouth, so we should listen more than we say.*
>
> Zeno of Citium

If our love is only a will to possess, it is not love.

Thich Nhat Hanh

Non-violence means avoiding not only external physical violence but also internal violence of spirit. You not only refuse to shoot a man, but you refuse to hate him.

Martin Luther King, Jr

The curious paradox is that when I accept myself just as I am, then I can change.

Carl Rogers

Don't worry that children never listen to you; worry that they are always watching you.

Robert Fulghum

Be like a river in generosity and giving help.
Be like a sun in tenderness and pity. Be like
night when covering others' faults. Be like the
dead when furious and angry. Be like the earth
in modesty and humbleness. Be like a sea in
tolerance. Be as you are.

Rumi

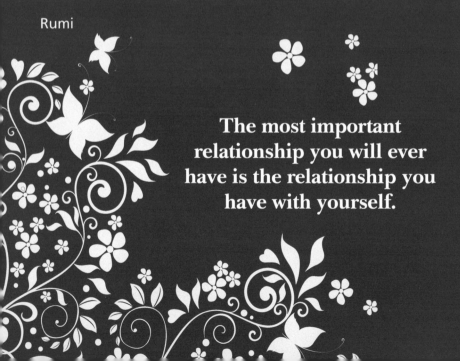

The most important
relationship you will ever
have is the relationship you
have with yourself.

The trance of unworthiness keeps the sweetness of belonging out of reach.

Tara Brach

Intimacy is the capacity to be rather weird with someone – and finding that that's OK with them.

Alain de Botton

Beware of total strangers and friends alike who shower you with comfortable sameness, and remain open to those who make you uneasy, for they are the true messengers of the future.

Rob Lebow

Treat people as if they were what they ought to be and you help them become what they are capable of being.

Goethe

Have patience with everything unresolved in your heart and try to love the questions themselves. Don't search for the answers which could not be given to you now because you would not be able to live them. And the point is, to live everything. Live the questions now. Perhaps then you will gradually, without even noticing it, live your way into the answers.

Rainer Maria Rilke

Never does the human soul appear so strong as when it forgoes revenge, and dares forgive an injury.

E.H. Chapin

Love teaches me I am everything;
Wisdom teaches me I am nothing.
Between the two my life flows.

Sri Nisargadatta

Kindness is more important than wisdom, and the recognition of that is the beginning of wisdom.

Theodore Rubin

To care for anyone else enough to make their problems one's own is ever the beginning of one's real ethical development.

Felix Adler

Those who love deeply never grow old; they may die of old age, but they die young.

Benjamin Franklin

When other people hurt us,
our instinct is to retreat away
from the world. But actually
it is only by engaging with
the world that we can ever
find true happiness.

Whatever affects one directly, affects all indirectly. I can never be what I ought to be until you are what you ought to be. This is the interrelated structure of reality.

Martin Luther King, Jr

*What comes
from the heart
goes to the heart.*

Samuel Taylor Coleridge

**The roots of resilience are to be found
in the felt sense of existing in the heart
and mind of an empathic, attuned, self-
possessed other.**

Diana Fosha

If science is to bring happiness and real progress to the world, it needs the warmth of man's heart just as much as the cold inquisitiveness of his brain.

Franz Winkler

Sometimes a person needs a story more than food to stay alive.

Barry Lopez

When we focus on ourselves, our world contracts as our problems and preoccupations loom large. But when we focus on others, our world expands. Our own problems drift to the periphery of the mind and so seem smaller, and we increase our capacity for connection – or compassionate action.

Daniel Goleman

When it's over, I want to say: all my life I was a bride married to amazement. I was the bridegroom, taking the world into my arms.

Mary Oliver

It hurts to care; the courage to care is the profoundest courage there is.

Julia Butterfly Hill

Could a greater miracle take place than for us to look through each others' eyes for an instant?

Henry David Thoreau

Too often we underestimate the power of a touch, a smile, a kind word, a listening ear, an honest compliment, or the smallest act of caring, all of which have the potential to turn a life around.

Leo Buscaglia

If a human disagrees with you, let him live. In a hundred billion galaxies, you will not find another.

Carl Sagan

Respond, don't react.
Listen, don't talk.
Think, don't assume.

Raji Lukkor

When you have the wisdom to truly understand a situation, compassion toward all parties involved is automatic, and compassion means that you automatically restrain yourself from any thought, word, or deed that might harm yourself or others.

Bhante Henepola Gunaratana

A real love letter is made of insight, understanding, and compassion. Otherwise it's not a love letter. A true love letter can produce a transformation in the other person, and therefore in the world. But before it produces a transformation in the other person, it has to produce a transformation within us. Some letters may take the whole of our lifetime to write.

Thich Nhat Hanh

It is in the shelter of each other that the people live.

Irish blessing

If you feel weak, think of all those in history who have wielded great power. Did it result in them being any happier, deep down, than someone without power?

At times our own light goes out and is rekindled by a spark from another person. Each of us has cause to think with deep gratitude of those who have lighted the flame within us.

Albert Schweitzer

Emotion is contagious.

Malcolm Gladwell

We have to work with people. We have to work with our fathers, our mothers, our sisters and brothers, our neighbours, and our friends. We have to do that because the people with whom we are associated in our lives provide the only situation that drives us to the spiritual search.

Chögyam Trungpa Rinpoche

Let everything happen to you
Beauty and terror
Just keep going
No feeling is final.

Rainer Maria Rilke

One kind word can warm three months of winter.

Japanese proverb

If we have no peace, it is because we have forgotten that we belong to each other.

Mother Teresa

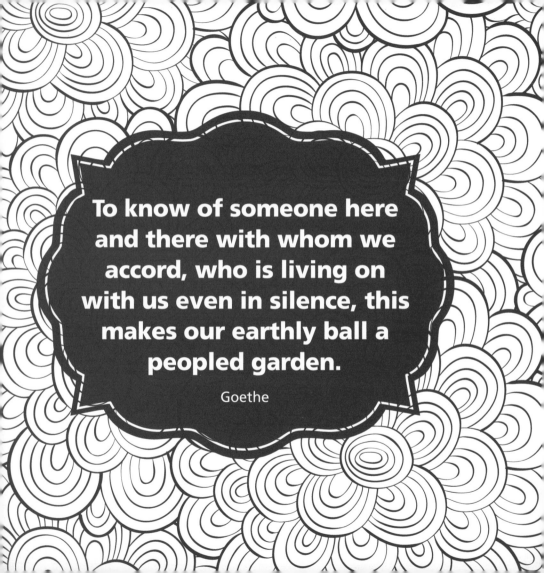

To know of someone here and there with whom we accord, who is living on with us even in silence, this makes our earthly ball a peopled garden.

Goethe

We should look for someone to eat and drink with, before looking for something to eat and drink.

Epicurus

We are all more intelligent than we are capable, and awareness of the insanity of love has never saved anyone from the disease.

Alain de Botton

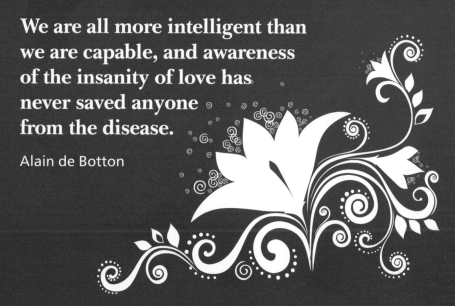

Be grateful for whoever comes, because each has been sent as a guide from beyond.

Rumi

5

Adversity & Acceptance

People have a hard time letting go of their suffering. Out of a fear of the unknown, they prefer suffering that is familiar.

Thich Nhat Hanh

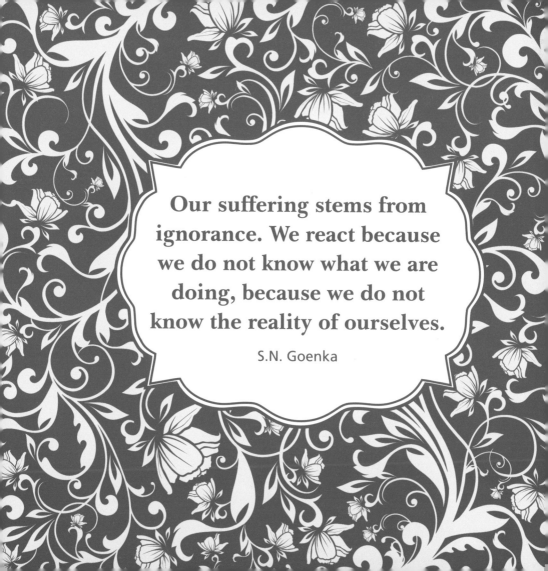

Our suffering stems from ignorance. We react because we do not know what we are doing, because we do not know the reality of ourselves.

S.N. Goenka

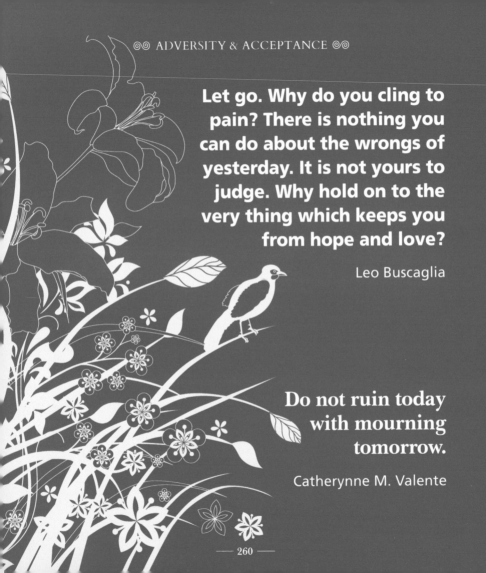

Let go. Why do you cling to pain? There is nothing you can do about the wrongs of yesterday. It is not yours to judge. Why hold on to the very thing which keeps you from hope and love?

Leo Buscaglia

Do not ruin today with mourning tomorrow.

Catherynne M. Valente

If a person's basic state of mind is serene and calm, then it is possible for this inner peace to overwhelm a painful physical experience. On the other hand, if someone is suffering from depression, anxiety, or any form of emotional distress, then even if he or she happens to be enjoying physical comforts, he or she will not really be able to experience the happiness that these could bring.

Dalai Lama

You get peace of mind not by thinking about it or imagining it, but by quietening and relaxing the restless mind.

Remez Sasson

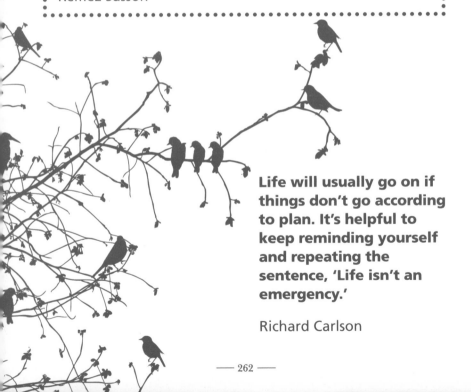

Life will usually go on if things don't go according to plan. It's helpful to keep reminding yourself and repeating the sentence, 'Life isn't an emergency.'

Richard Carlson

Perhaps all the dragons in our lives are princesses who are only waiting to see us act, just once, with beauty and courage.

Rainer Maria Rilke

People will do anything, no matter how absurd, to avoid facing their own soul.

Carl Gustav Jung

**Silence fertilizes the deep
place where personality grows.
A life with a peaceful centre
can weather all storms.**

Norman Vincent Peale

Serenity is not freedom from the storm,
but peace amid the storm.

**You carry in yourself
all the obstacles necessary
to make your realization
perfect. If you discover a
very black hole, a thick
shadow, be sure there is
somewhere in you a great light.
It is up to you to know how to
use the one to realize the other.**

Sri Auribindo

Courage is what you earn when you've been through the tough times and you discover they aren't so tough after all.

Malcolm Gladwell

No life is so hard that you can't make it easier by the way you take it.

Ellen Glasgow

In hard times, grieve not too much – appreciate the rhythm that controls men's lives.

Archilochus

The anticipated rarely happens, while the unexpected is bound to occur.

Sri Nisargadatta

The future depends on what we do in the present.

Mahatma Gandhi

It makes no sense to worry about things you have no control over because there's nothing you can do about them, and why worry about things you do control? The activity of worrying keeps you immobilized.

Wayne Dyer

One of the best protections against disappointment is to have a lot going on.

Alain de Botton

In the carriages of the past you can't go anywhere.

Maxim Gorky

The truth is that our finest moments are most likely to occur when we are feeling deeply uncomfortable, unhappy or unfulfilled. For it is only in such moments, propelled by our discomfort, that we are likely to step out of our ruts and start searching for different ways or truer answers.

M. Scott Peck

Worry is a misuse of imagination.

Dan Zadra

I come into the peace of wild things who do not tax their lives with forethought of grief. I come into the presence of still water. And I feel above me the day-blind stars waiting with their light. For a time I rest in the grace of the world, and am free.

Wendell Berry

Stress is caused by being 'here' but wanting to be 'there' or being in the present but wanting to be in the future.

Eckart Tolle

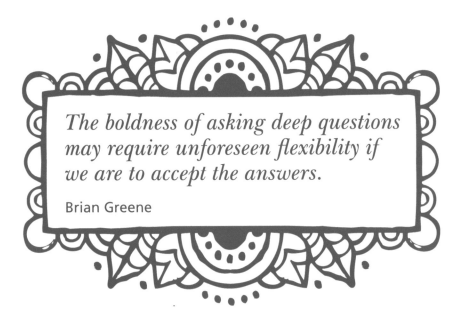

The boldness of asking deep questions may require unforeseen flexibility if we are to accept the answers.

Brian Greene

Anxiety is a thin stream of fear trickling through the mind. If encouraged, it cuts a channel into which all other thoughts are drained.

Arthur Somers Roche

Those times of depression tell you that it's either time to get out of the story you're in and move into a new story, or that you're in the right story but there's some piece of it you are not living out.

Carol S. Pearson

**We'll weather the weather,
Whatever the weather,
Whether we like it or not.**

John Ruskin

Even a god cannot change the past.

Agathon

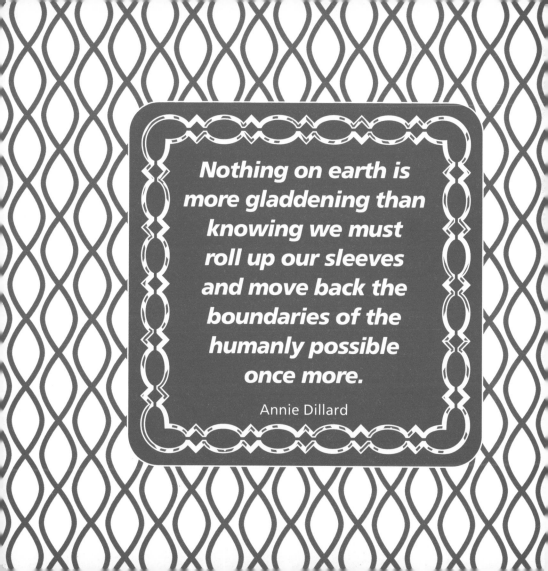

Nothing on earth is more gladdening than knowing we must roll up our sleeves and move back the boundaries of the humanly possible once more.

Annie Dillard

You can never worry your way to enlightenment.

Terri Guillemets

When we are unable to find tranquillity within ourselves, it is useless to seek it elsewhere.

François de La Rochefoucauld

What counts is not the enormity of the task, but the size of the courage.

Matthieu Ricard

Adversity has the effect of eliciting talents which, in prosperous circumstances, would have lain dormant.

Horace

When you become good at the art of letting sufferings go, then you'll come to realize what you were dragging around with you. And for that, no one else other than you was responsible.

Bhagwan Shree Rajneesh

Some days there won't be a song in your heart. Sing anyway.

Emory Austin

If you see a whole thing it seems that it's always beautiful. Planets. Lives. But close up a world's all dirt and rocks. And day to day, life's a hard job; you get tired; you lose the patterns.

Ursula K. Le Guin

That the birds of worry and care fly over your head, this you cannot change, but that they build nests in your hair, this you can prevent.

Chinese proverb

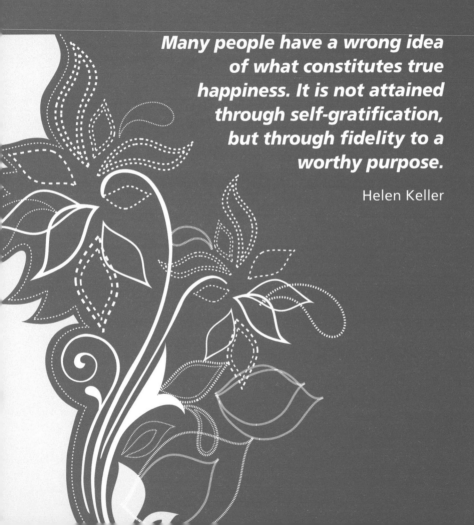

Many people have a wrong idea of what constitutes true happiness. It is not attained through self-gratification, but through fidelity to a worthy purpose.

Helen Keller

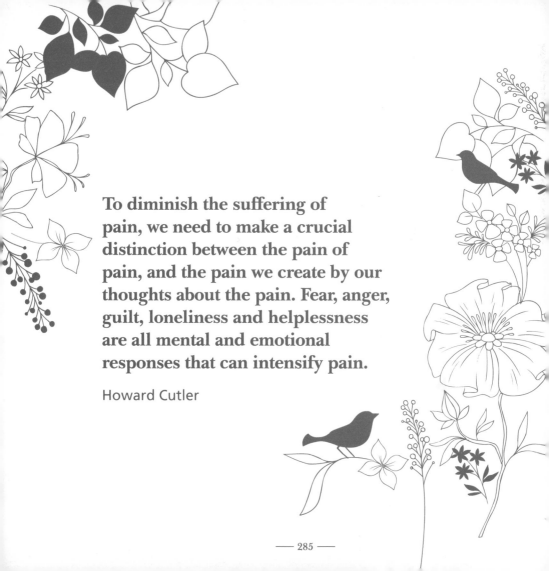

To diminish the suffering of pain, we need to make a crucial distinction between the pain of pain, and the pain we create by our thoughts about the pain. Fear, anger, guilt, loneliness and helplessness are all mental and emotional responses that can intensify pain.

Howard Cutler

EXERCISE: *Waves on a beach*

This exercise is designed to help you when you find it difficult to deal with negative thought patterns.

1 Imagine you are sitting on a peaceful beach. It is warm, and you are wearing a bathing suit. The tide brings warm waves lapping all around you.

2 Bobbing in the waves are clear glass bottles. Each of the bottles contains a written 'message' which is one of your own thoughts. Some of these thoughts are positive, and some of them are negative. They are all mixed up together. Just let them all come in on the tide, and go back out on the tide. 'Read' each thought as it passes by you, just by recognizing that it belongs to you: you wrote the message in the bottle. Try not to react to the message itself, just observe each one.

3 As the tide turns and begins to go out, focus your attention on one positive message that you wrote with your mind. Pluck that bottle from the sea, and hold onto it. Allow the tide to take all the other bottles back out to sea. Observe them all, getting ever smaller, as the tide retreats.

4 Now perform a real-world action which relates to the message in the bottle that you chose to keep hold of. It might be as simple as running a hot bath, taking the dog for a walk, or phoning a friend. The important thing to recognize is that you can choose which thoughts to act upon, and which to allow to recede beyond the horizon.

**We shape clay into a pot,
but it is the emptiness inside
that holds whatever we want.**

Lao-Tzu

**What we call evil is simply ignorance
bumping its head in the dark.**

Henry Ford

Grief has limits, whereas apprehension has none. For we grieve only for what we know has happened, but we fear all that possibly may happen.

Pliny the Younger

We are all faced with a series of great opportunities brilliantly disguised as impossible situations.

Charles R. Swindoll

Old times never come back and I suppose it's just as well. What comes back is a new morning every day in the year, and that's better.

George E. Woodberry

The basic root of happiness lies in our minds; outer circumstances are nothing more than adverse or favourable.

Matthieu Ricard

**Some of your hurts
you have cured,
And the sharpest you still
have survived,
But what torments of grief
you endured
From the evil which
never arrived.**

Ralph Waldo Emerson

Life is expressed in a perpetual sequence of changes. The birth of the child is the death of the baby, just as the birth of the adolescent is the death of the child.

Arnaud Desjardins

The moment we want to be something we are no longer free.

J. Krishnamurti

God made the world round so we would never be able to see too far down the road.

Isak Dinesen

Great spirits have always encountered violent opposition from mediocre minds.

Albert Einstein

Nothing ever gets anywhere. The earth keeps turning round and gets nowhere. The moment is the only thing that counts.

Jean Cocteau

*Somehow our devils
are never quite
what we expect
when we meet them
face to face.*

Nelson DeMille

**If you want to conquer the
anxiety of life, live in the
moment, live in the breath.**

Amit Ray

**The moon
broken again and again on the sea
so easily mends**

Choshu

All changes, even the most longed for, have their melancholy; for what we leave behind is a part of ourselves.

Anatole France

We each need to make our lion's roar – to persevere with unshakable courage when faced with all manner of doubts and sorrows and fears – to declare our right to awaken.

Jack Kornfield

For me, it is far better to grasp the Universe as it really is than to persist in delusion, however satisfying and reassuring.

Carl Sagan

I tell you the past is a bucket of ashes.

Carl Sandburg

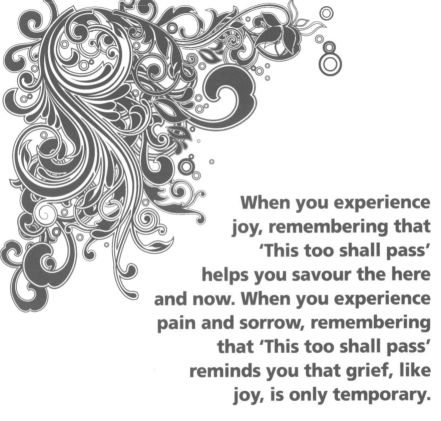

When you experience joy, remembering that 'This too shall pass' helps you savour the here and now. When you experience pain and sorrow, remembering that 'This too shall pass' reminds you that grief, like joy, is only temporary.

Joey Green

Sooner or later, everyone sits down to a banquet of consequences.

Robert Louis Stevenson

There are no wrong turns, only unexpected paths.

Mark Nepo

Mindfulness is the direct path for the purification of beings, for the overcoming of sorrow and lamentation, for the disappearing of pain and grief, for the attainment of the Way, for the realization of nirvana.

Shakyamuni Buddha

The purpose of life is to be defeated by greater and greater things.

Rainer Maria Rilke

To escape the self-trap, to be sane and decent and awake and whole – that is all that matters.

Vernon Howard

*When people are at a loss, the guide
ferries them over. When one is
awake, one ferries oneself.*

Hui-Neng

**You can do anything
you think you can.
This knowledge is
literally the gift of the
gods, for through it
you can solve every
human problem.**

Robert Collier

There are only facts, i.e., occurrences in space and time.

John Anderson

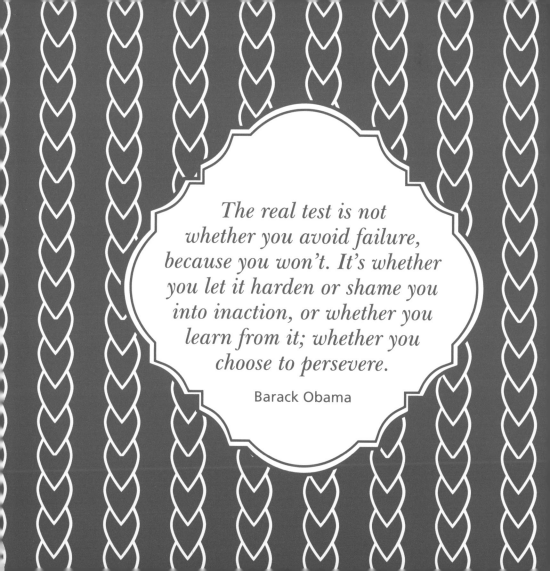

The real test is not whether you avoid failure, because you won't. It's whether you let it harden or shame you into inaction, or whether you learn from it; whether you choose to persevere.

Barack Obama

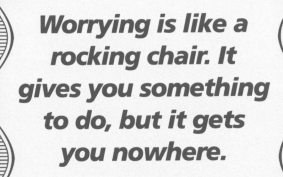

Worrying is like a rocking chair. It gives you something to do, but it gets you nowhere.

Glenn Turner

Perfection of character is this: to live each day as if it were your last, without frenzy, without apathy, without pretence.

Marcus Aurelius

Suffering usually relates to wanting things to be different from the way they are.

Allan Lokos

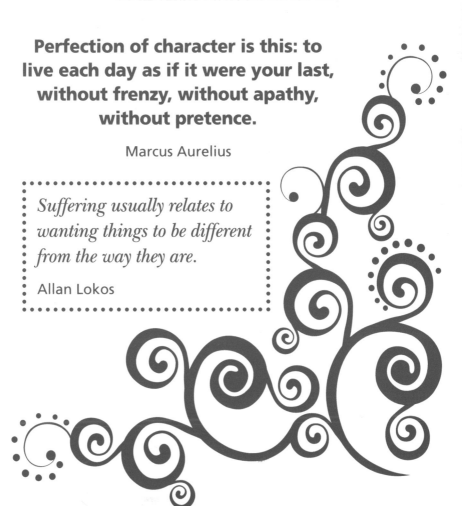

Our lives are lived in intense and anxious struggle, in a swirl of speed and aggression, in competing, grasping, possessing and achieving, forever burdening ourselves with extraneous activities and preoccupations.

Sogyal Rinpoche

In order to complete our amazing life journey successfully, it is vital that we turn each and every dark tear into a pearl of wisdom, and find the blessing in every curse.

Anthon St Maarten

Not being understood
may be taken as a sign
that there is much in one
to understand.

Alain de Botton

By regarding things and clinging to them as 'I' or 'mine', bondage occurs. When bound to something, we get stuck in it, just like being stuck in prison.

Buddhada-sa Bhikkhu

Begin at once to live, and count each separate day as a separate life.

Seneca

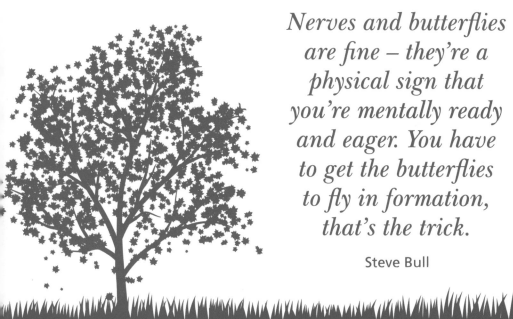

Nerves and butterflies are fine – they're a physical sign that you're mentally ready and eager. You have to get the butterflies to fly in formation, that's the trick.

Steve Bull

Storms make oaks take deeper roots.

George Herbert

One can make a day of any size, and regulate the rising and setting of his own sun and the brightness of its shining.

John Muir

Developing skill in facing and effectively handling the various 'weather conditions' in your life is what we mean by the art of conscious living.

Jon Kabat-Zinn

Time will explain it all. He is a talker, and needs no questioning before he speaks.

Euripides

When one door closes another door opens; but we so often look so long and so regretfully upon the closed door, that we do not see the ones which open for us.

Alexander Graham Bell

*If things go wrong,
don't go with them.*

Roger Babson

Let us spend one day as
deliberately as Nature, and not be
thrown off track by every nutshell and
mosquito's wing that falls on the rails.

Henry David Thoreau

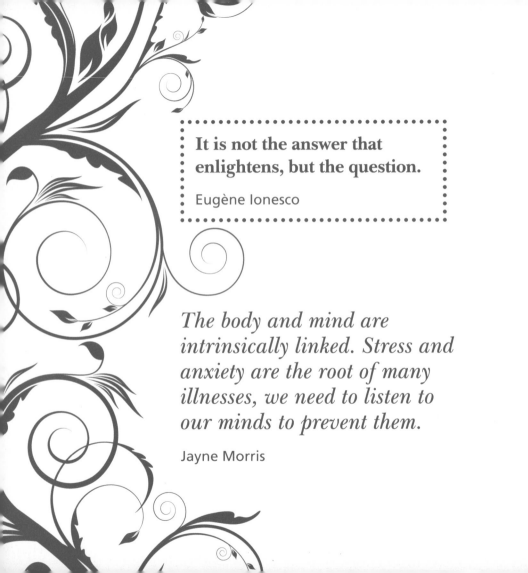

It is not the answer that enlightens, but the question.

Eugène Ionesco

The body and mind are intrinsically linked. Stress and anxiety are the root of many illnesses, we need to listen to our minds to prevent them.

Jayne Morris

The colour of springtime is in the flowers; the colour of winter is in the imagination.

Terri Guillemets

It is a common habit to blame life upon the environment. Environment modifies life but does not govern life. The soul is stronger than its surroundings.

William James

Keep some measure in the joy you take in luck, and the degree you give way to sorrow.

Archilochus

Drag your thoughts away from your troubles . . . by the ears, by the heels, or any other way you can manage it.

Mark Twain

Today, like every other day, we wake up empty and frightened.
Don't open the door to the study and begin reading.
Take down a musical instrument.

Rumi

*Don't let yesterday
use up too much
of today.*

Cherokee proverb

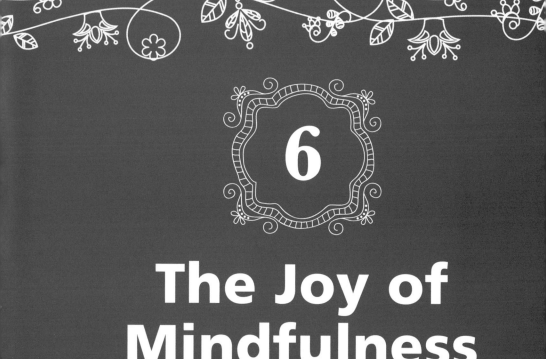

6

The Joy of Mindfulness

*Dedicate yourself to the good you deserve and
desire for yourself. Give yourself peace of mind.
You deserve to be happy. You deserve delight.*

Mark Victor Hansen

All the art of living lies in a fine mingling of letting go and holding on.

Havelock Ellis

In actuality, misery is a moment of suffering allowed to become everything.

Mark Nepo

If you meditate, sooner or later you will come upon love. If you meditate deeply, sooner or later you will start feeling a tremendous love arising in you that you have never known before.

Osho

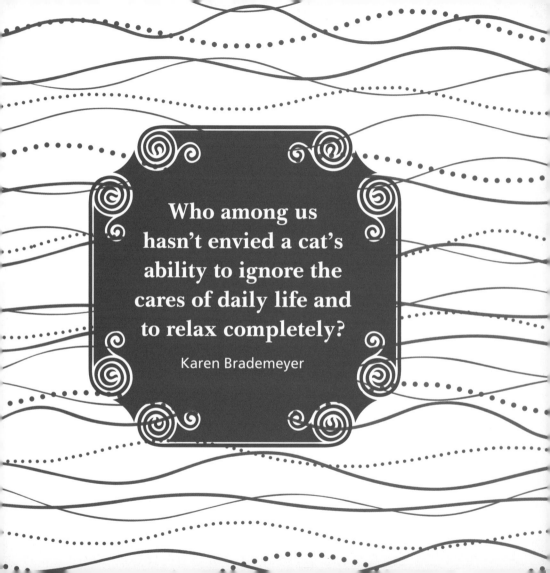

Who among us hasn't envied a cat's ability to ignore the cares of daily life and to relax completely?

Karen Brademeyer

Everything you do can be done better from a place of relaxation.

Stephen C. Paul

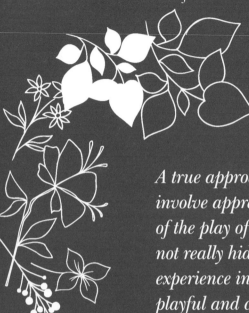

A true approach to mysticism would involve appreciating the mysteriousness of the play of phenomena, which is not really hidden from you. Mystical experience in this second sense is often playful and contains a great deal of humour. There is something that is not quite solemn and solid but rather operates on the level of the delight of experiencing things as they are.

Chögyam Trungpa Rinpoche

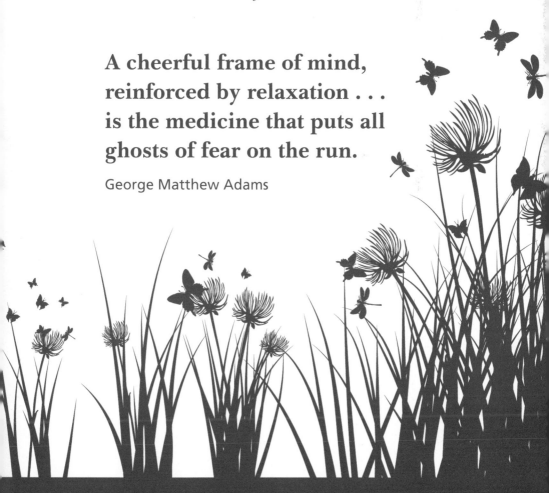

A cheerful frame of mind,
reinforced by relaxation . . .
is the medicine that puts all
ghosts of fear on the run.

George Matthew Adams

Everything is based on mind, is led by mind, is fashioned by mind. If you speak and act with a pure mind, happiness will follow you, as a shadow clings to a form.

Buddha

> For peace of mind, we need to resign as general manager of the universe.
>
> Larry Eisenberg

The time to relax is when you don't have time for it.

Jim Goodwin and Sydney J. Harris

*Laughter relaxes.
And relaxation
is spiritual.*

Bhagwan Shree Rajneesh

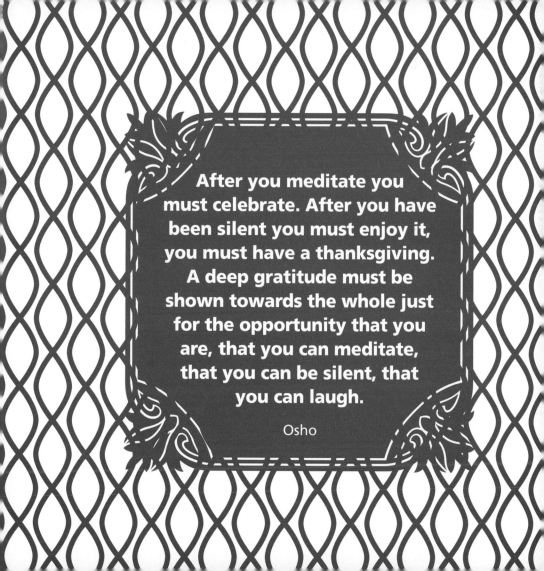

After you meditate you must celebrate. After you have been silent you must enjoy it, you must have a thanksgiving. A deep gratitude must be shown towards the whole just for the opportunity that you are, that you can meditate, that you can be silent, that you can laugh.

Osho

Thoughts aren't fact, so don't take them seriously.

Ruby Wax

Personally, I don't think there's intelligent life on other planets. Why should other planets be any different from this one?

Bob Monkhouse

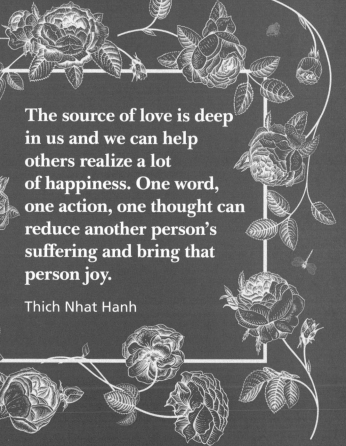

The source of love is deep in us and we can help others realize a lot of happiness. One word, one action, one thought can reduce another person's suffering and bring that person joy.

Thich Nhat Hanh

The personal life deeply lived always expands into truths beyond itself.

Anaïs Nin

A peaceful mind generates power.

Norman Vincent Peale

Half our life is spent trying to find something to do with the time we have rushed through life trying to save.

Will Rogers

**Joy does all things
   without concern:
For emptiness, stillness,
   tranquillity, tastelessness,
Silence, and non-action
Are the root of all things.**

Chuang Tzu

Yes, risk-taking is inherently failure-prone. Otherwise, it would be called sure-thing-taking.

Tim McMahon

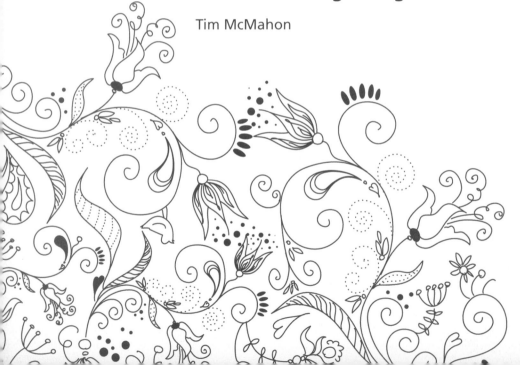

There are many wonderful things, and nothing is more wonderful than man.

Sophocles

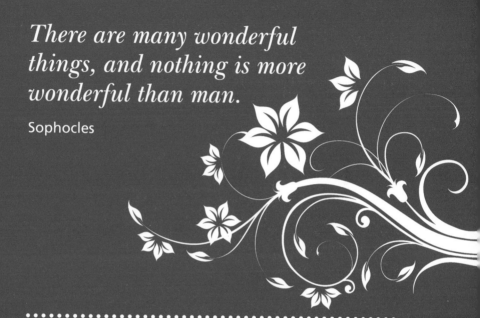

The passing moment is all that we can be sure of; it is only common sense to extract its utmost value from it.

W. Somerset Maugham

Waste not fresh tears over old griefs.

Euripides

Life is no 'brief candle' for me. It is a sort of splendid torch which I have got hold of for a moment, and I want to make it burn as brightly as possible before handing it on to the future generations.

George Bernard Shaw

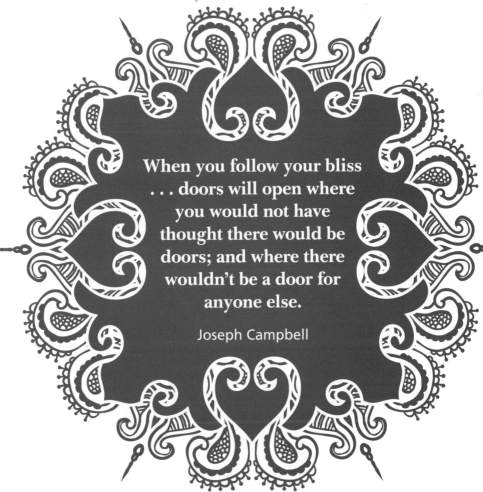

When you follow your bliss
. . . doors will open where
you would not have
thought there would be
doors; and where there
wouldn't be a door for
anyone else.

Joseph Campbell

After silence, that which comes nearest to expressing the inexpressible is music.

Aldous Huxley

Don't go around saying the world owes you a living. The world owes you nothing. It was here first.

Mark Twain

There is no better means of attainment to the spiritual life than by continually beginning again.

St Francis de Sales

Living the past is a dull and lonely business; looking back strains the neck muscles, causing you to bump into people not going your way.

Edna Ferber

I slept and dreamed that life was joy.
I awoke and saw that life was service.
I acted and, behold, service was joy.

Rabindranath Tagore

All meditation procedures stress concentration of the mind, bringing the mind to rest on one item or one area of thought. Do it strongly and thoroughly enough, and you achieve a deep and blissful relaxation, called jhana. It is a state of such supreme tranquillity that it amounts to rapture.

Bhante Henepola Gunaratana

*Mindfulness of the body
leads to nirvana.*

Shakyamuni Buddha

***Rejoice in the things that
are present; all else is
beyond thee.***

Michel de Montaigne

Do not waste a single moment.
This is my principle. Therefore,
my daily life is extremely busy.
However, that is how I feel joy.

Kyoshu Sama

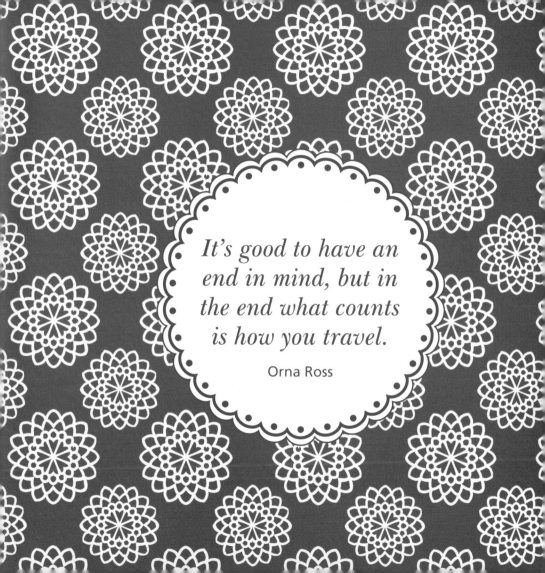

It's good to have an end in mind, but in the end what counts is how you travel.

Orna Ross

If the doors of perception were cleansed, everything would appear to man as it is, infinite. For man has closed himself up, till he sees all things thro' narrow chinks of his cavern.

William Blake

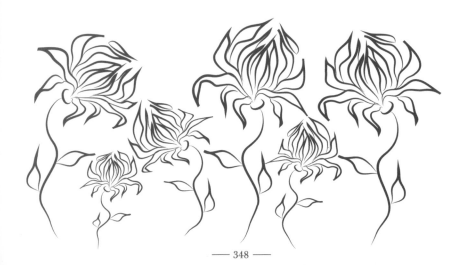

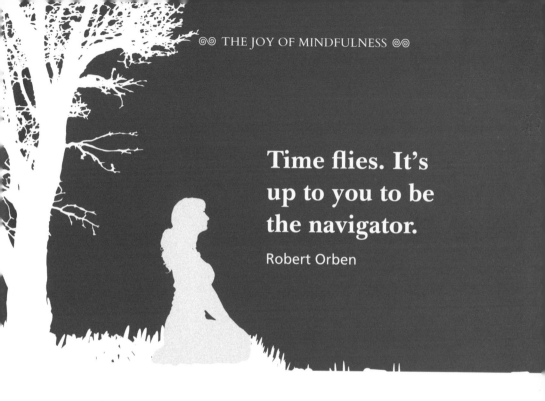

Time flies. It's up to you to be the navigator.

Robert Orben

You can't wring your hands and roll up your sleeves at the same time.

Pat Schroeder

We rarely hear the inward music, but we're all dancing to it nevertheless.

Rumi

It will not always be easy, but it will always be beautiful.

Charlotte Eriksson

*Bury me
next to friendly people.
I like to talk a lot.*

Hal Kaplan

**Not knowing when
the dawn will come,
I open every door.**

Emily Dickinson

A perfect summer day is when the sun is shining, the breeze is blowing, the birds are singing, and the lawn mower is broken.

James Dent

Life is too important to be taken seriously.

Oscar Wilde

Like a child standing in a beautiful park with his eyes shut tight, there's no need to imagine trees, flowers, deer, birds, and sky; we merely need to open our eyes and realize what is already here, who we already are – as soon as we stop pretending we're small or unholy.

Bo Lozoff

In all things of nature there is something of the marvellous.

Aristotle

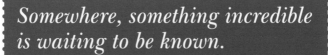

Somewhere, something incredible is waiting to be known.

Carl Sagan

Sometimes your only available transportation is a leap of faith.

Margaret Shepherd

Fear less, hope more; eat less, chew more; whine less, breathe more; talk less, say more; love more, and all good things will be yours.

Swedish proverb

Truth is not in some far-distant place; it is the looking at 'what is'.

J. Krishnamurti

Dare to dream! If you did not have the capability to make your wildest wishes come true, your mind would not have the capacity to conjure such ideas in the first place.

Anthon St Maarten

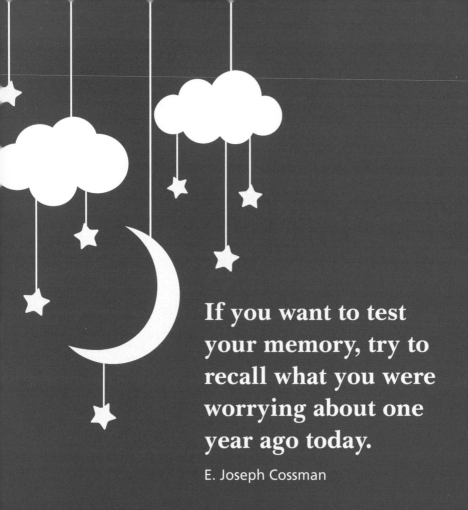

If you want to test your memory, try to recall what you were worrying about one year ago today.

E. Joseph Cossman

Reverie is not a mind vacuum. It is rather the gift of an hour which knows the plenitude of the soul.

Gaston Bachelard

It pays to keep an open mind, but not so open your brains fall out.

Carl Sagan

Slow down and enjoy life. It's not only the scenery you miss by going too fast – you also miss the sense of where you are going and why.

Eddie Cantor

Inner peace can be seen as the ultimate benefit of practising patience.

Allan Lokos

I have found my greatest moments of joy and peace just sitting in silence, and then I take that joy and peace with me out into the world.

Holly Mosier

We are the miracle of force and matter
making itself over into imagination and will.
Incredible. The Life Force experimenting
with forms. You for one. Me for another.
The Universe has shouted itself alive.
We are one of the shouts.

Ray Bradbury

Silence is a fence around wisdom.

German proverb

When I was younger, I could remember anything, whether it had happened or not.

Mark Twain

Children have neither past nor future; they enjoy the present, which very few of us do.

Jean de la Bruyère

Purpose is the place where your deep gladness meets the world's needs.

Frederick Buechner

**Be content with what you have;
Rejoice in the way things are.
When you realize there is
nothing lacking,
The whole world belongs
to you.**

Lao-Tzu

If we could see a single flower clearly, our whole life would change.

Buddha

Education is simply the soul of a society as it passes from one generation to another.

G.K. Chesterton

Home is not where you live, but where they understand you.

Christian Morganstern

Those who are awake live in a state of constant amazement.

Shakyamuni Buddha

You normally have to be bashed about a bit by life to see the point of daffodils, sunsets and uneventful nice days.

Alain de Botton

Wisdom begins in wonder.

Socrates

Whatever happens, we always have a fundamental positive quality about our experience of life. Such faith could be said to be the source of an almost magical performance. If a person relies on that confidence, it is almost as though she is going to perform a miracle, and she is taking quite a chance that the miracle might not happen. However . . . she does what she has to do, and the miracle does happen.

Chögyam Trungpa Rinpoche

If you treat every situation as a life and death matter, you'll die a lot of times.

Dean Smith

Seize from every moment its unique novelty, and do not prepare your joys.

André Gide

If you're hung up on nostalgia, pretend today is yesterday and just go out and have one hell of a time.

Art Buchwald

Let everyone sweep in front of his own door, and the whole world will be clean.

Johann Wolfgang von Goethe

The key to knowing joy is being easily pleased.

Mark Nepo

You can judge your age by the amount of pain you feel when you come in contact with a new idea.

Pearl S. Buck

Every evening I turn my worries over to God. He's going to be up all night anyway.

Mary C. Crowley

We don't stop playing because we grow old; we grow old because we stop playing.

George Bernard Shaw

Only man clogs his happiness with care, destroying what is with thoughts of what may be.

John Dryden

Intuition: the feeling you know something when you know nothing.

Marty Rubin

Nothing in the world is permanent, and we're foolish when we ask anything to last, but surely we're still more foolish not to take delight in it while we have it.

W. Somerset Maugham

Gratitude unlocks the fullness of life.

Melody Beattie

I got the blues thinking of the future, so I left off and made some marmalade. It's amazing how it cheers one up to shred oranges and scrub the floor.

D.H. Lawrence

Cherish wisdom as a means of travelling from youth to old age, for it is more lasting than any other possession.

Bias of Priene

It is surprising how contented
one can be with nothing definite
– only a sense of existence. My
breath is sweet to me. O how I
laugh when I think of my vague
indefinite riches. No run on my
bank can drain it, for my
wealth is not possession
but enjoyment.

Henry David Thoreau

Trust in dreams, for in them is the hidden gate to eternity.

Kahlil Gibran

It stands to reason that anyone
who learns to live well will die well.
The skills are the same: being present
in the moment, and humble, and brave,
and keeping a sense of humour.

Victoria Moran

It is only possible to live happily-ever-after on a day-to-day basis.

Margaret Wander Bonnano

All religions will pass, but this will remain: simply sitting in a chair and looking at the distance.

V.V. Rozanov

If you come from a place of love then you are free and fear dispels itself into nothing if you live in the moment – in the present – then you don't fear because you can let all the good, the miracles, in.

Cat Forsley